W9-AEO-990

Springer Series on ADULTHOOD and AGING

Series Editor: Bernard D. Starr, Ph.D.
Advisory Board: Paul D. Baltes, Ph.D., Jack Botwinick, Ph.D., Carl Eisdorfer, Ph.D., M.D., Donald E. Gelfand, Ph.D., Lissy Jarvik, M.D., Ph.D., Robert Kastenbaum, Ph.D., Neil G. McCluskey, Ph.D., K. Warner Schaie, Ph.D., Nathan W. Shock, Ph.D., and Asher Woldow, M.D.

Vol. 1 **Adult Day Care** Philip G. Weiler et al. O.P.

Vol. 2 **Counseling Elders and Their Families:** Practical Techniques for Applied Gerontology John J. Herr and John H. Weakland

Vol. 3 **Becoming Old:** An Introduction to Social Gerontology John C. Morgan

Vol. 4 **The Projective Assessment of Aging Method (PAAM)** Bernard D. Starr, Marcella Bakur Weiner, and Marilyn Rabetz

Vol. 5 **Ethnicity and Aging** Donald E. Gelfand and Alfred J. Kutzik, with 25 contributors

Vol. 6 **Gerontology Instruction in Higher Education** David A. Peterson and Christopher R. Bolton O.P.

Vol. 7 **Nontraditional Therapy and Counseling with the Aging** S. Stansfeld Sargent et al.

Vol. 8 **The Aging Network:** Programs and Services, 2nd ed. Donald E. Gelfand

Vol. 9 **Old Age on the New Scene** Robert Kastenbaum, with 29 contributors

Vol. 10 **Controversial Issues in Gerontology** Harold J. Wershow, with 36 contributors

Vol. 11 **Open Care for the Aging:** Comparative International Approaches Virginia C. Little

Vol. 12 **The Older Person as a Mental Health Worker** Rosemary McCaslin, with 11 contributors

Vol. 13 **The Elderly in Rural Society:** Every Fourth Elder Raymond T. Coward and Gary R. Lee, with 16 contributors

Vol. 14 **Social Support Networks and the Care of the Elderly:** Theory, Research, and Practice William J. Sauer and Raymond T. Coward, with 17 contributors

Vol. 15 **Managing Home Care for the Elderly:** Lessons from Community-Based Agencies Anabel O. Pelham and William F. Clark, with 10 contributors

Vol. 16 **A Basic Guide to Working with Elders** Michael J. Salamon

Vol. 17 **Communication Skills for Working with Elders** Barbara Bender Dreher

Vol. 18 **Ethnic Dimensions of Aging** Donald E. Gelfand and Charles M. Barresi, with 22 contributors

Vol. 19 **Exercise Activities for the Elderly** Kay Flatten, Barbara Wilhite, and Eleanor Reyes-Watson

Vol. 20 **Recreation Activities for the Elderly** Kay Flatten, Barbara Wilhite, and Eleanor Reyes-Watson

Vol. 21 **The Facts on Aging Quiz** Erdman B. Palmore

Kay Flatten was born in Kansas City and lived and studied in Topeka, Kansas, earning a B.Ed. from Washburn University of Topeka. In 1967, she entered Indiana University and began studying human movement in the field of biomechanics. She received M.S. and P.E.D. degrees, and went on to teach at the University of Wisconsin–La Crosse, the University of Indianapolis, and most recently Iowa State University. Her interest in exercise and movement patterns of older adults developed when she cared for her grandmother. Dr. Flatten now teaches courses on human movement and aging and she coordinates the undergraduate gerontology minor at Iowa State University. She and Dr. Wilhite consult on the use of the Exercise Activities and Recreation Activities for the Elderly concept and materials in various settings.

Barbara Wilhite, Ed.D., a native of Atlanta, Georgia, holds advanced degrees in Recreation and Special Education. She earned a Certificate in Gerontology from the University of Georgia. Her area of interest is therapeutic recreation and she is currently certified as a Therapeutic Recreation Specialist by the National Council for Therapeutic Recreation Certification. Her practical experiences include working with juvenile offenders, individuals with physical and mental disabilities, individuals with psychological impairments, and older adults. She has worked in both the community and institutional setting. She currently teaches within the Department of Recreation, Southern Illinois University, Carbondale. Dr. Wilhite is active in various professional organizations related to gerontology and recreation and often shares her expertise through workshops and presentations.

Eleanor Reyes-Watson was born in the Philippines and educated there and in the U.S. She received a B.Ed. from Purdue University and B.A. and M.A. degrees from the University of Wyoming. Studies in dance and an interest in the elderly led to her work with senior citizens, for several years, in a special program in St. Paul, Minnesota. In 1984, she responded to a request to develop materials for friendly visiting. While writing *Exercise Activities for the Elderly*, she studied in the Gerontology Program at Iowa State University. She is currently the volunteer coordinator for the Octagon Center for the Arts in Ames, Iowa.

Recreation Activities for the Elderly

Kay Flatten, P.E.D.
Barbara Wilhite, Ed. D.
Eleanor Reyes-Watson, M.A.

SPRINGER PUBLISHING COMPANY
NEW YORK

Springer Publishing Company, Inc.
536 Broadway
New York, NY 10012

88 89 90 91 92 / 5 4 3 2 1

Library of Congress Cataloging-in-Publication Data

Flatten, Kay.
   Recreation activities for the elderly / Kay Flatten, Barbara
Wilhite, Eleanor Reyes-Watson.
      p.   cm. — (The Springer series on adulthood and aging)
   Companion v. to: Exercise activities for the elderly / Kay
Flatten, Barbara Wilhite, Eleanor Reyes-Watson.
   Includes bibliographies
   ISBN 0-8261-6030-1 (pbk.)
   1. Aged—Recreation.   2. Social work with the aged.   I. Wilhite.
Barbara Cathryn, 1952-   II. Reyes-Watson, Eleanor.
III. Flatten, Kay.   Exercise activities for the elderly.   IV. Title.
V. Series.
GV447.F58 1988
613.7'0880565—dc19   88-3263
                                          CIP

Contents

PREFACE.. vii
INTRODUCTION... ix

PART I: USING THE ACTIVITIES EFFECTIVELY

1. Characteristics and Needs of the Elderly..............   3

2. Learning About Recreation...........................   11

3. Conducting the Activities...........................   23

4. Coordinating the Program............................   37

PART II: ACTIVITIES

5. Special Features of the Program.....................   49
    Assessing recreation interests.....................   55
    Community resource referral........................   59

6. Crafts...   63
    Making bread dough crafts..........................   63
    Decorating bread dough crafts......................   67
    Sock dolls...   71
    Decorated jars.....................................   75
    Quiet book...   79
    Block printing.....................................   83
    References and resources...........................   87

7. Games..   93
    Simple card games..................................   93
    Guessing games.....................................   97
    Dominoes... 101
    Solitaire.. 107
    Indoor golf.. 113
    Finger shuffleboard................................ 117
    References and resources........................... 121

8. Hobbies.. 123
        Fun with books... 123
        Fun with puzzles... 127
        Our feathered friends.................................... 133
        Astronomy.. 137
        Indoor gardening... 143
        Music appreciation....................................... 149
        References and resources................................. 157

9. Literature... 159
        Letter writing... 159
        Poetry gems.. 163
        Poetry to music.. 167
        Word pyramids.. 171
        Reading aloud.. 175
        Spoken scrapbook... 179
        References and resources................................. 181

10. Remembering the Past..................................... 183
        Oral history introduction................................ 183
        School days.. 187
        Health problems.. 191
        Travel... 195
        Jobs... 199
        Creating a book.. 203
        References and resources................................. 209

APPENDICES

Appendix A. Audiovisuals....................................... 213
Appendix B. Equipment List..................................... 217
Appendix C. Leader Training Program............................ 221
Appendix D. Job Description.................................... 225

Preface

We must love what we are, or else we doom
The sovereign self of slavery and hate.
Yet, love we must the what we may become
Lest self-indulgence substitute for fate
And wall us up in such a tiny room
That sun can shed no warmth, early or late.*

--Will C. Jumper

This book began at the request of social service agency professionals
delivering programs to elderly populations. These agency professionals
were involved in the delivery of nutritional and medical services
to many older persons, but they felt the psychological needs of "fun
and friendship" were not being adequately addressed. They were
especially concerned about the lack of social contact among people
who seldom leave their residences, regardless of the reason. This
concern--and the ensuing request for program materials to meet this
concern--were directed to Drs. Barbara Wilhite and Kay Flatten and
graduate assistant Eleanor Reyes, specialists in recreation and exercise
for older populations.

The intent of the program was: (1) to attract committed persons for
one-on-one contact with older individuals; (2) to train these leaders
in specific encounter techniques and structured activities suitable
for special populations; and (3) to continue to motivate these service
providers to work with the frail elderly on a regular basis. Once
in the leadership role, the goal was to direct the time to mutually
enjoyable activities and avoid prolonged conversation on negative
aspects of the older person's current situation.

The program includes training material for use by professionals in
the gerontology field, directors of volunteer programs in various

*Jumper, Will C. From Time Remembered. Orange, California: Foothills
Press, 1977, p. 37.

vii

settings, and community or institutional exercise and recreation specialists. In addition, <u>Recreation Activities for the Elderly</u>, and its companion volume <u>Exercise Activities for the Elderly</u>, provide specific activity plans for use in working with frail elderly.

The program can be used by educators and social service providers alike. Colleges with gerontology curricula can use the program as a laboratory for learning about the needs and characteristics of frail elderly. Agencies offering friendly visiting can use the program to supplement their activities. Professional staff in residential care or community settings can add these activities to their existing recreation and exercise programming.

The authors wish to thank Ann Charles and Bev Kruempel for planting the seed of the original concept. Elizabeth Smith, Susan Scott, Faye Burke, Liz Selk, Barb Wacker, Elaine James, and Faith Balch were invaluable in trying out the original concept within their various professional capacities. Helping to put the concept on paper were Charm Price, Nancy Spiess, Janet Rickey, Darrell Simmermaker, Barb Wing, Rob Watson, and Hilary Matheson. Gratitude and respect are felt for our professional colleagues Dr. Richard MacNeil, Betty Bocella, Dr. Jean Keller, Dr. Caroline Weiss, Jane Ann Stout, Dr. Janet MacLean, Dr. Rosabel Koss, Janet Pomeroy, Bernice Bateson, Dr. Helen Mills, and Dr. Helen LeBaron Hilton, who were generous with their time and critical insight in reviewing the entire program prior to field testing. The recreation activities in this book were reviewed by Dr. Richard MacNeil, Betty Bocella, Dr. Jean Keller, Dr. Caroline Weiss, and Jane Ann Stout. The authors would also like to acknowledge the assistance of various professionals who have contributed indirectly to the development of this text through information and expertise shared in the literature and via workshops and presentations.

We have been fortunate in receiving timely support from the Department of Health and Human Services, Administration on Aging, to study further the homebound elderly and design appropriate program intervention. This support allowed the materials to be field-tested in three communities, with extensive evaluation of their impact on frail elderly, volunteer leaders, and human service agencies. In addition, the Department of Physical Education and Leisure Studies and the Research Institute for Studies in Education at Iowa State University and the Department of Recreation at Southern Illinois University provided support and encouragement to the authors. A special thanks to Mr. William Whipple and the Hall Foundation of Cedar Rapids, Iowa, who also funded a portion of the project-development costs.

Finally, we wish to thank the senior volunteers and home-centered elderly who have touched our lives, and in so doing have made this program a process of love and mutual friendship for all.

Introduction

WHAT IS THE RECREATION PROGRAM?

This manual is one of a two-volume set, including a companion book, Exercise Activities for the Elderly. Both books are designed to be used by staff or volunteers and their directors when preparing to deliver the activities to frail older persons.

Part I in each volume includes information needed to prepare the leader to use the activities. This knowledge base addresses the characteristics and needs of a frail elderly person, as well as leadership techniques and methods for working with such individuals. Basic information about recreation is also included in **Part I** of this manual. Likewise, information on exercise theory is found in **Part I** of Exercise Activities for the Elderly.

Part II in each book contains the activities. These are organized into interest areas (units). There are six activity plans for each interest area. Each activity plan is named and includes the purpose of the activity, benefits of the activity, and complete directions on how to prepare for and lead the activity. References and resources are listed at the end of each unit to allow the reader to enrich the area.

A unique feature of the program is contained in the common activity plans. Each recreation unit will begin with the same "get acquainted" activity plan (Activity Plan 1) to help the leader assess the recreation interests of the elder. Each unit will include a community resource referral activity plan (Activity Plan 8). During this session the leader will inform the elder about services and programs in the community which may be of use in pursuing the unit topic or in maintaining self-sufficiency. The ninth session in each unit is reserved for the elder and leader to enjoy an activity of their own choosing.

WHERE CAN THE RECREATION PROGRAM BE USED?

There are three logical settings for the program. These range from friendly visiting in home settings to hospital, nursing home, and other institutional programs, and finally to university curricula. The program was originally designed as a resource for the Retired Senior Volunteer Program (RSVP) Friendly Visiting Programs. RSVP is a program under ACTION, established in 1969 to help older Americans take advantage of opportunities for voluntary service in their communities. The purposes of RSVP include mobilization of a large potential volunteer force, the provision of meaningful roles for retired persons, and the correction of stereotypes about older people.

The recreation activities in this manual contribute to the impact of home visitation. They promote renewed involvement in the mainstream of life, an increased awareness and widening concept of what recreation is, a reawakening of creative impulses, the encouragement of social involvement, and the provision of meaningful roles. Recreation program materials developed for use by paraprofessionals during home visits strengthen friendly visiting programs by providing meaningful content as well as structure. These materials can direct visitation time away from conversations about losses toward positive, self-improving activities.

The recreation program can also be a part of the services provided by hospitals, nursing homes, and other residential settings. In such cases the service providers may be volunteers, as described earlier, or activities may be led by staff or family members. Since the materials are designed to be used in a one-to-one format, staff/client ratios may not allow for 1-hour sessions per client per week. In order to offer this basic contact, staff may want to train family members to deliver the program. Families have a strong desire to help, and visiting loved ones in an institutional setting can become difficult when the stay is extended. Eventually families exhaust all ideas and conversations. "How are you feeling" only goes so far, and the resident does not have a variety of experiences once the daily routine has been shared. Paid staff can offer training to family and volunteers at various times to accommodate working visitors and can prepare a brochure to give family members upon admission of the resident.

Universities are increasing the number of courses designed to help students prepare for careers in gerontology. The recreation and exercise program can be adapted for use in such curricula. The manuals can be used as the texts for such courses. Students could meet twice weekly for 1 hour to complete training in 4 weeks. Students would then be matched with elderly persons to visit once a week. The class would continue to meet once a week for the remaining 9 weeks of the semester. These class sessions would be used to discuss experiences and continue with learning activities.

The instructor can assign the units to students and establish a resource library for the students to use in conducting sessions. Students and the instructor can work together to plan a party at the end of the semester, to draw the elders into a social activity.

An interesting adaptation of this course is to invite well elderly to enroll. In this way a college student can have experience working with two levels of aging, the well elderly, still in the mainstream of society, and the frail elderly.

WHO ARE THE LEADERS OF THE RECREATION PROGRAM?

Recreation activities are a logical extension of social services as presently provided. The best service delivery model seems to involve volunteers and leaders working within already existing networks of service to the elderly.

A survey conducted by the Bureau of Census for the federal agency for volunteerism, ACTION, has revealed that about 7 million persons age 55 and older were engaged in volunteer work. One out of every five persons age 55 to 64 and one out of seven age 65 and older contributed an average of 8 hours of service weekly to volunteer activities in their communities. The value of these services is estimated to be $11.6 billion. With current government budgetary cutbacks, the volunteer segment of our society plays a crucial role in servicing frail elderly. This is especially necessary when the delivered service is free.

Using a 1985 homemaker hourly wage rate of $10.54 from a not-for-profit visiting nurse association in Ames, Iowa, it is possible to calculate the cost in salary alone to deliver a recreation unit. The time commitment for one unit would include the following:

Hours	Breakdown
8	8 hours training
9	1-hour session for 9 weeks
9	1-hour weekly meeting of leaders for 9 weeks
4.5	1/2-hour preparation for each of the activity sessions
30.5	total hours
@ $10.54	hourly rate
$321.47	cost for training and leading one unit

Since training is only needed once, the cost to deliver subsequent units would be less. The annual cost for one leader to deliver the program would be $1,349.12. The value and worth of a volunteer leader is substantiated by these cost estimates.

This program can be adapted for use by other service recipients of all ages, such as the developmentally disabled and the chronically ill. The program can also be used in different settings, such as extended-care facilities and community leisure service organizations. Volunteers may also represent various ages and backgrounds. One such recommendation is the use of these activities in an intergenerational program.

Regardless of how closely the training and activity materials and the service delivery approach are followed, the underlying goals of the program should not be compromised. These goals are:

    to promote physical and mental well-being through fun and enjoyment;

    to maintain maximum independence and integration into the community;

    to provide feelings of self-worth to the leader and elder; and

    to direct activity time away from conversations about losses toward positive, self-improving activities.

Studies regarding the benefits gained by home-centered elderly through friendly visiting programs have been conducted. Tendencies for improvement in life satisfaction, perceived health status, and social isolation were found when home visits were received over an extended period. Friendly visitor programs can be a vital link between the isolated elderly and community services available for their physical, mental, and social welfare. In addition, if visitors are trained to recognize signs of stress in aged persons in their own homes, the program may prevent a crisis leading to relocation of the aged person, a stress which is fatal to many elderly persons.

UNIT DESCRIPTIONS

Crafts - The craft activities presented in this unit are mainly of the construction type, involving the use of materials. The activities are nontechnical, inexpensive, and easily completed within one or two visits. Sample craft projects include bread dough art and sock doll projects.

Games - The games presented in this unit range from pencil and paper and table games to modified versions of shuffleboard and golf. Some emphasize mental activities, while others are more physical.

Hobbies - This unit contains discussions on a variety of ways to pursue activities providing personal satisfaction and pleasure. Various art, reading, and craft activities presented in other units are expanded upon in this unit. Sample hobbies include puzzles, music appreciation, astronomy, gardening, and bird watching.

Literature - This unit contains a variety of passive activities involving reading and writing skills. Examples of activities include book reviewing, poetry reading and writing, letter writing, crossword puzzles, reading aloud, word games, and the creation of a personal scrapbook.

Remembering the Past - This unit is ideal for use when participants resist structured activity. Each session has a brief reading from a senior's autobiography. The sessions focus on topics including school days, jobs, medical remedies, and travel. The unit culminates with the making of a book about the elder's discussions during the unit.

The following describes units which may be found in the accompanying volume Exercise Activities for the Elderly.

Exercises for Strength - This unit consists of a series of exercises designed to work specific joints and muscles. An accompanying manual shows the leader and elder what the exercises look like when performed, and also which muscles are strengthened. The exercises begin on an easy level and move to higher levels of difficulty with each session. The number of repetitions and the difficulty of the exercises are noted on each activity plan. The elder records progress during the unit.

Exercises for Arthritis, Diabetes, and Parkinson's Disease - Lack of activity sometimes leads to complications, especially among those who have chronic conditions. The gentle exercises in this unit encourage the nonactive individual to move, stretch, and improve breathing. The goal of the unit is to improve flexibility and prevent loss of muscle strength, while learning how to manage the target conditions.

Exercises for Special Purposes - Activities in this unit are designed to help maintain the flexibility needed to carry out tasks of daily living. Mild exercises for the neck, hands, arms, shoulders, legs, and feet, are included, as well as exercises to do in bed when confined. Two special sessions are devoted to strengthening the internal muscles that help in breathing and bladder control.

PART I
Using the Activities Effectively

CHAPTER 1

Characteristics and Needs of the Elderly

Said the little boy, "Sometimes I drop my spoon."
Said the little old man, "I do that too."
The little boy whispered, "I wet my pants."
"I do that too," laughed the little old man.
Said the little boy, "I often cry."
The old man nodded, "So do I."
"But worst of all," said the boy, "it seems
Grown-ups don't pay attention to me."
And he felt the warmth of a wrinkled old hand.
"I know what you mean," said the little old man.*

--Shel Silverstein

UNDERSTANDING AGING

One of the first questions that probably occurs to a leader is "Why is this person frail?" The older person may be experiencing one or more problems associated with being confined to the home or institution. Being familiar with these characteristics will help the leader determine the needs of the elder and make the activity more helpful and enjoyable. Aging is a universal experience and the process results in changes which have a strong impact on various aspects of a person's life. How an individual adapts to change can be crucial to emotional and physical well-being. The following concerns are the result of the normal aging process or are some common reasons elderly people may become frail.

1. Sensory Loss or Decline

Some problems of the frail elderly are directly related to changes in the ability to see, hear, taste, smell, touch. Because the senses

*"The Little Boy and the Old Man," from A Light in the Attic, by Shel Silverstein. Copyright ©1981 by Evil Eye Music, Inc. Reprinted by permission of Harper & Row, Publishers, Inc.

are a person's link with the outside world, they are crucial to how one perceives others and the outside world.

2. Slower Reaction Time

Reaction time increases as a person ages, but reaction time for simple tasks does not increase as much as reaction time for complicated tasks.

3. Tendency to Fatigue

The tendency to fatigue easily may be the result of several factors. Prolonged or sudden illness, emotional stress, worry, and the like all put a strain on a person's body. Inactivity is sometimes necessary for healing, but too much inactivity results in a weakened body. Activity of a proper intensity can be extremely beneficial both physically and mentally. Becoming involved in an activity that will take the focus away from a person's usual routine or problems can be a relief and a reassurance that one still has the capacity to do, think, and feel.

4. Chronic Illness

Even though a majority of older people have few restrictions on their general activity level, most do have some kind of chronic problem during old age. The problems, however, are minor or the person learns to adjust to them. Chronic conditions that most commonly affect the aged are

> arthritis
> heart conditions
> high blood pressure (or hypertension)
> visual and hearing problems
> loss of teeth
> aphasia (speech disorder due to brain cell damage)
> diabetes
> asthma and emphysema
> memory and attention span declines
> cancer
> Parkinson's disease

Chronic illness may affect people in a variety of ways. Problems with hearing and vision, lack of strength, coordination and flexibility all limit the ability to move. Lack of mobility has an impact on the ability to take care of daily needs. Contact with other people may become more limited. Sometimes the overall effect of multiple long-term chronic illnesses is emotional problems which make it difficult to function normally.

5. Acute Illness

Examples of acute illnesses are: the flu, a cold, a cut, or a broken bone, etc. When an older person has an acute illness, the impact can often be severe. For example, when an older person receives a cut, there is greater chance of infection because of reduced circulation. A disorder such as flu can be serious for somone who does not have the reserve capacity to fight it off. Acute illness may have the effect of causing a person to be temporarily bedridden, disrupting daily routines and requiring assistance with daily tasks.

6. Lack of Transportation

Mobility outside the home is very important to a person's sense of independence. Lack of transportation makes it difficult to provide for one's needs and forces one to depend on others to satisfy those needs. This may result in feelings of frustration, resentment, and isolation.

Some of the reasons for lack of transportation include limited finances, living in an area that is not serviced by a public transportation system, or having a disability that makes it difficult to travel without the aid of specially equipped vehicles.

7. Emotional Sensitivity

Emotionally related problems include the loss of roles such as that of a spouse, mother, sibling, friend, or professional, and the loss of loved ones. For many older people, fear limits involvement. Feeling safe in one's environment adds incentive to become involved in the community.

8. Financial Problems

Many older people live on limited or fixed incomes. Today money buys many things--even good health. Limited income can affect a person's mental and emotional well-being. Participation in some social events or educational activities, such as travel, special classes, lectures, and concerts, is sometimes limited by finances.

NEEDS OF THE ELDERLY

Understanding the characteristics common to frail elderly individuals will be helpful in identifying their needs. In general, these needs can be grouped as physical, social, intellectual, emotional, or spiritual. Needs that can be specifically addressed by the recreation program are:

  (a) the need to continue using body muscles and joints to prevent
      loss of strength and flexibility;
  (b) the need to feel safe and secure while carrying out physical
      activities;
  (c) the need to maintain contact with a variety of people;
  (d) the need to maintain and acquire friends;
  (e) the need for opportunities to learn new skills and develop
      new interests;

(f) the need to maintain self-esteem; and
(g) the need to feel useful.

To test your knowledge of the characteristics of the elderly and to point out potential prejudices in your perceptions of older persons, complete the following quiz. Answers for the quiz can be found on page 9. This quiz was developed by Dr. Erdman Palmore at the Center for the Study of Aging and Human Development at Duke University.

FACTS ON AGING[*]

T   F   1. The majority of old people (past age 65) are senile (i.e., defective memory, disoriented, or demented).

T   F   2. All five senses tend to decline in old age.

T   F   3. Most old people have no interest in, or capacity for, sexual relations.

T   F   4. Lung capacity tends to decline in old age.

T   F   5. The majority of old people feel miserable most of the time.

T   F   6. Physical strength tends to decline in old age.

T   F   7. At least one-tenth of the aged are living in long-stay institutions (i.e., nursing homes, mental hospitals, homes for the aged, etc.).

T   F   8. Aged drivers have fewer accidents per person than drivers under age 65.

T   F   9. Most older workers cannot work as effectively as younger workers.

T   F   10. About 80% of the aged are healthy enough to carry out their normal activities.

T   F   11. Most old people are set in their ways and unable to change.

T   F   12. Old people usually take longer to learn something new.

T   F   13. It is almost impossible for most old people to learn new things.

[*]Adapted from Palmore, Erdman. Facts on aging: A short quiz. The Gerontologist, 1977; 17(4), 315-320.

T   F   14.   The reaction time of most old people tends to be slower than reaction time of younger people.

T   F   15.   In general, most old people are pretty much alike.

T   F   16.   The majority of old people are seldom bored.

T   F   17.   The majority of old people are socially isolated and lonely.

T   F   18.   Older workers have fewer accidents than younger workers.

T   F   19.   Over 15% of the U.S. population are now age 65 or over.

T   F   20.   Most medical practitioners tend to give low priority to the aged.

T   F   21.   The majority of older people have incomes below the poverty level (as defined by the federal government).

T   F   22.   The majority of old people are working or would like to have some kind of work to do (including housework and volunteer work).

T   F   23.   Older people tend to become more religious as they age.

T   F   24.   The majority of old people are seldom irritated or angry.

T   F   25.   The health and socioeconomic status of older people (compared to younger people) in the year 2000 will probably be about the same as now.

REFERENCES AND RESOURCES

ACTION. The value of volunteer services in the United States. Pamphlet #3530.4, Stock #0456-000-00015-1, 1976. Washington, DC: U.S. Government Printing Office.

Birren, J. E., & Schaie, K. W. (Eds.). Handbook of the psychology of aging. New York: Van Nostrand Reinhold, 1977.

Bogart, A. G., & Larson, L. An evaluation of two visiting programs for elderly community residents. International Journal of Aging and Human Development, 1983; 17(4), 267-279.

Carroll, K. (Ed.). Compensating for sensory loss. Minneapolis, MN: Ebenezer Center for Aging and Human Development, 1978.

Crandall, R. C. Gerontology: A behavioral science approach. Reading, MA: Addison-Wesley, 1980.

Cummings, E., & Henry, W. In L. Troll (Ed.), Continuations: Adult development and aging. Monterey, CA: Brooks/Cole, 1982.

Ernst, M., & Shore, H. Sensitizing people to the processes of aging: The in-service educator's guide. Denton, TX: Dallas Geriatric Research Institute, 1977.

Jarvick, L. F. (Ed.). Aging into the 21st century. New York: Gardner Press, 1978.

Jumper, W. C. From time remembered. Orange, CA: Foothills Press, 1977.

Morris, W. W., & Hades, I. M. (Eds.). Hoffman's daily needs and interests of older people. Springfield, IL: Charles C. Thomas, 1983.

Mulligan, M. A., & Bennett, R. Development and evaluation of a friendly visitor program for the community aged. International Journal of Aging and Human Development, 1977; 8(1), 43-66.

National Council on the Aging. Fact book on aging: A profile of America's older population. Washington, DC: NCOA Research and Evaluation Department, 1978.

_____. Working with the at-risk older person: A resource manual. Washington, DC: NCOA, 1981.

Palmore, E. Facts on aging: A short quiz. The Gerontologist, 1977; 17(4), 315-320.

Retired Senior Volunteer Program: Operation handbook. No. 4405.92, August, 1983. Washington, DC: U.S. Government Printing Office.

Silverstein, S. A light in the attic. New York: Harper & Row, 1981.

Smith, E. L. The aging process and benefits of physical activities. In Research and practical activity programs for the aging. Pre-convention Symposium and Workshop Papers, American Alliance of Health, Physical Education, Recreation, and Dance, 1982.

Troll, L. E. Continuations: Adult development and aging. Monterey, CA: Brooks/Cole, 1982.

U.S. Department of Health, Education and Welfare. Working with older people: A guide to practice, vol. 1. Rockville, MD: U.S. Government Printing Office, 1978.

U.S. Public Health Service, Health Resource Administration. <u>Limitations of activity and mobility due to chronic conditions</u>. Vital and Health Statistics, Data from the National Health Series 10, No. 96. DHEW (HRA)75-1523. Rockville, MD: National Center for Health Statistics, 1974.

Key to the Quiz on Page 6.

All odd numbered items are false; all even numbered items are true.

CHAPTER 2

Learning About Recreation

Tell me what you are busy about,
and I will tell you what you are.

--Goethe

Recreation is viewed as a personal response prompted by the desire to satisfy needs. It is not just an activity but how one thinks and feels about the activity. There are several key ideas which describe the nature of the recreation experience:

Recreation is a pleasurable experience: Enjoyment is derived from the activity itself and there may also be delayed satisfactions. Enjoyment is not the only value derived from the recreation experience, but this value should always be present.

Recreation involves voluntary choice: The decision to participate in a recreational activity lies with the elder. Recreation is an experience that cannot be forced on the elder; no one can be ordered to enjoy an activity. One is free to choose, continue, or discontinue.

Recreation is a highly individualized experience: It is person-centered. The emphasis is on the elder--how he/she feels--not on the activity per se.

Recreation requires participation: It is activity, not inactivity. The activity, however, can range in intensity.

Recreation provides balance: It usually involves a change of pace or focus--gives a sort of balance to one's life.

Recreation involves the total person: It can enhance the elder's mental, emotional, physical, social, and spiritual well-being.

Recreation is broad in concept: The types of recreation are as numerous as human interests and desires. It involves all ages, capabilities, and intensities of activity.

VALUE OF RECREATION TO THE ELDER

Recreation activities can meet many needs of the home-centered individual. They can foster a channel of communication and enhance the desire to seek social contacts; serve as a method of health maintenance and restoration and assist in monitoring one's condition; and encourage intellectual and creative development and mental alertness. Recreation can also enable the home-centered individual to become more independent and self-confident. Through participation in recreation activities, the elder can discover resources within himself/herself. Other possible benefits derived from the recreation experience are listed below (Murphy & Howard, 1977; p. 116).*

PHYSICAL   INTELLECTUAL

Relief of tension   Mastery
Relaxation   Discovery
Exercise   Learning
Coordination   New experience
Muscle tone   Insight
Rejuvenation   Problem solving
Fitness   Self-awareness

PSYCHOLOGICAL   SOCIAL

Reflection   Friendships
Challenge   Companionship
Accomplishment   Trust
Excitement   Cultural sharing
Pleasure   Concern for others
Self-expression   Belonging
Anticipation   Appreciation

SPIRITUAL

Knowledge expansion
Revelation
Release
Contemplation
Meditation
Wonderment

*Murphy, James F., & Howard, Dennis R. Delivery of community services. Philadelphia, PA: Lea & Febiger, 1977. Used by permission.

GOALS FOR THE LEADER

The leader's involvement with the elder should be geared toward developing positive attitudes about oneself and recreation experiences. The leader also assists the elder to become involved in the community and in self-help programs. Goals for the leader include the following (Halberg, 1985; p. 186):[*]

to serve as a recreation and social resource for the participant;

to encourage and support the pursuit of former, current, and potential interests, abilities, and skills;

to provide opportunities for physical, intellectual, emotional, and social challenges;

to provide opportunities for enjoyment and satisfaction;

to provide experiences which support the development of feelings of self-worth and usefulness;

to stimulate social interaction; and

to facilitate independence through the development of personal recreation and social skills, positive attitudes, and resources.

Suggestions for leading recreation activities with the participant are as follows (Des Moines Area Community College, 1983):

Encourage the elder to do only what he/she can handle. Small successes will have to be achieved before moving on to larger ones. Let the elder set the pace of the activity since it is often easy to become fatigued and discouraged.

Keep relaxed and present the activity as pleasantly as possible. Treat mistakes lightly!

The leader should understand the techniques of a particular activity but need not be an expert. Don't expect or demand from the elder a higher quality of performance than is possible.

Constantly look for clues to the elder's interest and ability which may lead to new activities.

The elder may be able to teach the leader some activities; be receptive to this.

*From K. J. Halberg, The role of the leisure services professional. In G. H. Maguire (Ed.), Care of the elderly: A health team approach. Boston: Little, Brown, ©1985. Used by permission.

ASPECTS OF RECREATION ACTIVITIES

When an elder engages in an activity, certain demands are required. That is, certain abilities and skills are required for the elder to do the activity. Action is required in three areas--physical, intellectual, and emotional--regardless of the type of activity. In addition, activities can possess certain social aspects. Many activities are also felt to contain spiritual aspects.

The better the leader understands the activities utilized during the session, the more likely that the elder will derive benefits from these activities. Breaking down the activity into its parts and examining the activity also helps the leader determine what abilities are necessary for successful participation. Some major considerations in each area of concern are presented below.

1. **Physical aspects**

    Is the full body involved or only part(s) of the body? Which part(s)?

    What type of manipulative movement is involved (throwing, catching, kicking, pulling, pushing, grasping, lifting, etc.)?

    What type of mobility is required (walking, balancing, twisting, bending, etc.)?

    What level of exertion is required?

    What degree of coordination of body parts is involved?

    How much endurance is necessary?

    What sensory demands are made (sight, hearing, touch, etc.)?

    What body position is required (sitting, lying, standing)?

2. **Intellectual aspects**

This may be the most important requirement of activity participation since the mind controls body movement as well as other aspects of participation.

    How many rules are required to do the activity? How complex are the rules?

    How much will the elder have to remember?

    What level of concentration is required to perform the activity?

    Are academic skills such as spelling, reading, and math required?

What degree of strategy is involved (the ability to analyze alternatives and make decisions)?

3. Emotional aspects

Generally, the leader should be concerned with what emotional reactions/responses are likely to be stimulated by the activity.

Does the activity release tension (stress)?

Does the activity allow the elder to communicate feelings?

Does the activity generally lead to fun?

Does frustration commonly arise from doing the activity?

How much creativity is possible?

Can the activity lead to self-esteem?

Is self-discipline necessary?

Is the activity stimulating? Exciting?

4. Social aspects

Is cooperation emphasized? Competition?

Does the activity involve being close to others? Physically touching?

Does the activity provide opportunity for interaction with the opposite sex?

How much verbal communication is required in the activity?

How structured is the activity?

What types of interactions occur (contact with the environment, contact with the leader, working individually)?

What amount of initiative is required?

5. Spiritual aspects

Does the activity pertain to a specific religion, faith, or denomination?

Does the activity provide opportunities to care for and serve others?

Does the activity have spiritual value in the aesthetic sense--beauty, awe, grandeur?

Does the activity promote a sense of being close to God?

Does the activity promote a sense of peace of mind?

SELECTION OF APPROPRIATE ACTIVITIES

For activities to be effective, they must meet the needs and interests of the elder. The activities utilized in the program units have been selected on the basis of general activity needs and interests (preferences) of the frail elderly population. In addition, activity selection has been based on practical considerations such as equipment, supplies, space, time, and costs. Other factors that have influenced activity selection include the age-appropriateness of the activity (Are the skills and social behaviors involved appropriate for the individual?) and access to materials and events (Does the elder have access to needed equipment or supplies in the home? Is transportation available to special events or settings to facilitate involvement in the activity?).

It is recommended, however, that the leader attempt to discover more specific needs and interests through personal interaction with the elder. The leader should be alert to the elder's physical condition, emotional and intellectual state, background (social, cultural, work, leisure, religious, environmental), activities of daily living performance and habits. This information can help the leader identify those needs and problems which can be aided through participation in certain activities. To determine interests, try to establish what ideas, people, places, or things in general catch the elder's attention. Then suggest activities related to these subjects. Ideally, actual selection of activities should be made by the elder. Therefore, allow as much input in this process as possible. Once the leader has become more familiar with the elder's needs and interests, some units and/or activities may not be entirely appropriate. Based on what has been learned, the activity may be modified or perhaps put aside for a later time.

ADAPTING RECREATION ACTIVITIES

The activities utilized in the program have been analyzed, providing a description of the activity for the leader to follow. In addition, the activity plan format provides information to help decide whether the elder's needs will be met and possible modifications for special conditions or situations. The activity description is broken down into materials and equipment needed, procedures, safety factors, special precautions, etc.

For the analysis to be more complete, however, the leader is urged to mentally separate the activity into its physical, social, emotional, intellectual, and spiritual aspects and consider how each of these aspects affects suitability of the activity for the elder. Activity adaptation, changing any aspect of an activity, is a direct result of activity analysis. By adapting activities when and where necessary, barriers to the elder's involvement can be eliminated or reduced. Activity adaptation enables and enhances participation.

The following guidelines are helpful when adapting activities to your own needs:

1. Base activity changes on the elder's strengths and weaknesses relative to the activity. Make adaptations to suit the elder's abilities rather than disabilities.

2. View adaptation as a temporary and transitional change in the original activity if possible.

3. Adapt only when necessary--if it is needed for participation, success, and enjoyment.

4. Whenever possible, include the elder in the process of developing activity adaptations. For example, simply ask, "How can you best do this?"

5. Keep the adapted activity as close to the original or standard version as possible.

6. Consider the elder's medical history and make sure adaptations are approved by medical personnel.

Some examples of ways to adapt activities are listed below.

1. **Material adaptation**

   Oversized writing instruments (pen, pencil, etc.)
   Blunt scissors (for safety); dual scissors (for assisting)
   Lightweight equipment (plastic, foam, etc.)
   Bowling aids (ramps, ball pusher, etc.)
   Blunt yarn needles
   Giant face cards; braille face cards
   Enlarged peg checker sets with raised squares

2. **Procedural/rule adaptation**

   Sit down (or lie down) rather than stand.
   Walk rather than run.
   Permit additional trials (strikes, throws, misses, etc.).
   Push rather than strike (or vice versa).
   Reduce time periods; provide additional rest periods.
   Reduce playing dimensions (size of court, etc.).

3. Skill sequences adaptation

There are times when the typical sequence for performing the activity may require modification. For example, when boiling an egg, one sequence might be to place the egg in the pot of boiling water. For safety reasons, this sequence could be changed with the participant initially placing the egg in the pot, filling the pot with cold water, placing it on the stove, and bringing the water to a boil. Another cooking example would be to place the food in the oven before turning it on. Typically, the oven is first preheated, but changing this sequence may facilitate a safer activity (Wehman & Schleien, 1981).

4. Lead-up activity adaptation

A lead-up activity is a simplified version of an activity or exercise that allows for practice in some skill of a game, sport, or hobby. The purpose of a lead-up activity is to prepare the elder for full participation in the original activity (Wehman & Schleien, 1981). In needlework, for example, modified activities could include the use of a lacing board with plastic needle attached to a nylon cord, a sewing block (large plastic box with holes) allowing a large plastic needle with rope attached to pass through, and sewing cards to learn basic movements necessary for sewing and embroidery (Wehman & Schleien, 1981; p. 84).[*]

5. Techniques for modifying the presentation of activities

Use simple wording.
Give only one direction at a time.
Give the direction and demonstrate the task, thus reinforcing the cue.
Use more than one sense (touch, sight, hearing, etc.) to teach a task.
Start instruction with simple and specific directions and tasks.

Specific conditions may require individualized modifications or precautions. Some general examples are listed below.

1. Visually impaired

Orient the individual to the activity and environment in which the activity is conducted; remove/minimize all hazards.
Use brightly colored objects.
Physically guide or assist the elder as needed.
Make use of available braille materials if appropriate.

[*]From Paul Wehman and Stuart Schleien, Leisure programs for handicapped persons: Adaptations, techniques, and curriculum. Austin, TX: Pro-Ed, 1981. Used by permission.

Use clear verbal instructions; speak in a normal voice.
Ensure adequate lighting.
Demonstrate by touch, taste, and smell.

2. Hearing impaired

Having a general outline of what will be covered in the activity
   written out in advance to share with the elder.
Speak normally and always face the elder, maintaining eye
   contact.
Use visual aids, including hand signals or gesturing.

3. Physically disabled

Perform the activity from a sitting rather than standing
position.
Periodically check floors to ensure they are free from hazards
   that might cause tripping or slipping.
Watch for signs of fatigue.
Make use of assistive devices/support systems if appropriate.
Pay attention to problems with balance or stability.
Stabilize the object in front of the elder.

4. Respiratory problems

Work space should be as dust-free as possible.
Avoid or reduce exposure to cold.
Avoid physical fatigue.
Make sure the activity area has adequate ventilation.

5. Heart/circulatory problems

Perform the activity from a chair or have a chair available
   in case a rest is needed.
Do not rush the elder; slow the tempo of the activity.
Have short activity periods followed by longer rest periods.
Use lightweight material to reduce strain; stick to prearranged
   time limits.
Avoid vigorous and sustained activities.
Make sure activity area has a stable temperature and adequate
   ventilation.

6. Arthritis/reconstructed joints

Don't use activities requiring a pressing-down motion.
Avoid or minimize need for small-muscle manipulation (such
   as required in a small needlepoint activity).
If joints appear inflamed or if pain and/or fatigue is evident,
   discontinue activity.
Provide frequent rest periods.
Work within limitations of range of motion.

7. Shorter attention span or memory

Repeat instructions.
Keep the instructions short.
Let the elder set the pace.

8. Aphasia

Allow the elder time to speak and gesture.
Use language that can be interpreted and answered easily.
Watch for signs of fatigue and limit time accordingly.

REFERENCES AND RESOURCES

Adams, R. C., Daniel, A. N., McCubbin, J. S., & Rullman, L. Games, sports and exercises for the physically handicapped (3rd ed.). Philadelphia: Lea & Febiger, 1982.

Austin, D. R., & Powell, L. G. Resource guide: College instruction in recreation for individuals with handicapping conditions. Bloomington, IN: Indiana University, 1980.

Black, K. Short-term counseling, A humanistic approach for the helping professions. Belmont, MA: Wadsworth, 1984.

Bullock, C. C., Wohl, R. E., Weboeck, T. E., & Crawford, A. M. Leisure is for everyone: Resource and training manual. Chapel Hill, NC: Curriculum in Recreation Administration, University of North Carolina at Chapel Hill, 1982.

Cormier, S. L., Cormier, W. H., & Weisser, R. J. Interviewing and helping skills for health professionals. Belmont, MA: Wadsworth, 1984.

Des Moines Area Community College. Activity director workshop manual. Estherville, IA: Iowa Lakes Community College, 1983.

Dixon, J. T. Adapting activities for therapeutic recreation service: Concepts and applications. San Diego, CA: San Diego State University, The Campanile Press, 1981.

Halberg, K. J. The role of the leisure services professional. In G. H. Maguire (Ed.), Care of the elderly. A health team approach (pp. 185-193). Boston: Little, Brown, 1985.

Hamill, C. M., & Oliver, R. C. Therapeutic activities for the handicapped elderly. Rockville, MD: Aspen Systems Corporation, 1980.

Jacobs, B. Senior centers and the at-risk older person. Washington, DC: National Institute of Senior Centers, the National Council on the Aging, 1980.

Keller, M. J. Planning social recreation activities for older adults.
Bloomington, IN: Indiana University, 1981.

Kraus, R. G., Carpenter, G., & Bates, B. J. Recreation leadership
and supervision. Philadelphia: Saunders College Publishing, 1981.

Labanowich, S., Andrews, N. B., & Pollock, J. M. Recreation for the
homebound aging. Lexington, KY: Department of Health, Physical
Education, and Recreation, University of Kentucky, 1978.

Loesch, L. C., & Wheeler, P. T. Principles of leisure counseling.
Minneapolis, MN: Educational Media Corporation, 1982.

McDowell, C. F. Leisure counseling: Selected lifestyle processes.
Eugene, OR: University of Oregon, Center of Leisure Studies, 1976.

Moran, J. M. Leisure activities for the mature adult. Minneapolis,
MN: Burgess Publishing, 1979.

Murphy, J. F., & Howard, D. R. Delivery of community leisure services:
A holistic approach. Philadelphia: Lea & Febiger, 1977.

Peterson, C. A., & Gunn, S. L. Therapeutic recreation program design
(2nd ed.). Englewood Cliffs, NJ: Prentice-Hall, 1984.

Sherrill, C. Adapted physical education and recreation (2nd ed.).
Dubuque, IA: Wm. C. Brown Co., 1981.

Shivers, J. S., & Fait, H. F. Recreational service for the aging.
Philadelphia: Lea & Febiger, 1980.

Simon, S. B., Howe, L. W., & Kirschenbaum, H. Values clarification:
A handbook of practical strategies for teachers and students. New
York: A & W Visual Library, 1978.

Stein, T. A., & Sessoms, H. D. Recreation and special populations
(2nd ed.). Boston: Holbrook Press, 1977.

Teaff, J. D. Leisure services with the elderly. St. Louis: Time
Mirror/Mosby College Publishing, 1985.

U.S. Department of Health, Education and Welfare. Activities
coordinator's guide. HE22.208; L85. Washington, DC: U.S. Government
Printing Office, 1978.

Wehman, P., & Schleien, S. Leisure programs for handicapped persons:
Adaptations, techniques, and curriculum. Austin, TX: Pro-Ed, 1981.

CHAPTER 3

Conducting the Activities

....the key to the success of any recreation and
exercise experience is in large measure the quality of
leadership. "There is no substitute for good leadership."*

--G. S. O'Morrow

BASIC CONCEPTS OF TEACHING AND LEARNING

To gain full enjoyment and satisfaction from the program, the
participant must have at least a minimal amount of skill and knowledge
of the activities. Thus, the leader's responsibilities often involve
teaching. As recreation activities are introduced, the leader must
teach the needed skills. Five basic concepts of teaching and learning
are highlighted below (Kraus, Carpenter, & Bates, 1981; Russell, 1986).

Awareness of individual differences: Each elder is an individual
and must learn in a unique way. As leaders become aware of the
differences among seniors, they will avoid a standardized approach
to teaching and will not expect all to learn the same things or
at the same rate.

Learning by doing: In general, the elder will learn best by doing.
This does not mean that the individual must be physically active.
The nature of the "doing" depends on the activity. For example,
learning about music may be based on listening to a lecture and
then to music--both physically passive acts; the individual,
however, is involved in "doing."

Reinforcement and feedback: This important concept maintains
that when the elder performs as desired, these actions should

*From Gerald S. O'Morrow, Therapeutic recreation, 2nd edition, p.
139. ©1980. Reprinted by permission of Prentice-Hall, Inc., Engelwood
Cliffs, New Jersey.

be encouraged so that they will be repeated. Once behaviors are well established, praise may be needed less often. This concept also emphasizes the importance of providing feedback to give some idea of progress. This feedback may include informing of needed corrections. The essential point is that positive reinforcement, with appropriate feedback, results in faster and more efficient learning.

Importance of personal meaning: People learn best that which has, or comes to have, personal meaning. The leader should thus help the elder realize how the activity skill or knowledge being taught is personally related and what benefits will be gained by learning the activity.

Existing knowledge: New information will be more easily learned if it is related to what is already known. This concept requires that the leader know what the senior has already learned about an activity.

GENERAL SUGGESTIONS FOR LEADING AN ACTIVITY

The key to the success of the program will be the ability of the leader to direct a variety of activities. The following are hints to consider:

Always try to be at ease, optimistic, and positive in manner; emphasize the positive, not the negative.

Break up the activity into small parts so that it will be easier to teach. Establish smaller goals which combine into larger ones.

Identify the basic purpose/intent of the activity and give reasons (or benefits) for doing the activity.

Never promise anything on which it is not possible to follow through.

Let interest and enthusiasm be contagious. Also have fun as a leader!

Participate in the activity to the extent possible. Encourage as much involvement as possible, allowing the elder the opportunity to lead when appropriate.

Try to foresee and eliminate unexpected barriers or conditions that may result in problems.

Treat the elder as an individual, recognizing individual values, interests, and abilities; show respect and help maintain dignity.

Do not be disappointed if there is initial suspiciousness or nonacceptance. With familiarity and trust, sincerity will be accepted.

STAGES OF AN ACTIVITY SESSION

Preparing for the activity: The leader should know the activity thoroughly. Sometimes this means practicing the activity in advance with another person or persons. Any equipment needed should be gathered, and other required pre-planning, as indicated on the activity plan, should be performed. Also, consider the space that will be needed to accommodate the activity. It is helpful to read one activity plan beyond. This will allow the leader to check out the resources and restrictions of the environment in advance. For example, building a bird feeder (Hobbies Unit) requires knowing if there will be a tree or deck on which to hang the feeder.

Try to prepare the elder by developing feelings of confidence about the activity. As the activity is described, try to find out what is already known; begin instruction at that point.

Explanation and demonstration: The leader should be in a position to be seen and heard. Instructions should be clear and brief but presented without rushing. The activity should be presented one step at a time. Demonstration of the activity is essential in most cases. Give the elder a chance to ask questions regarding the directions; however, try to avoid lengthy explanations. Remember, the best learning occurs during involvement; get the senior involved as soon as possible.

Encourage and support participation during every stage of the session. Think of learning as sharing and interacting rather than directing and controlling. The explanation and demonstration stage will be most meaningful when the senior has some input.

Practice: Let the elder do the activity, guiding efforts and correcting when necessary. As the activity is performed, make sure the steps and procedures are understood. Remember to provide encouragement and feedback.

Evaluation: No activity will go perfectly without potential for further improvement. Evaluation consists of thinking about strengths and weaknesses of the activity. The leader relies primarily on observing and writing down significant aspects of the session. The leader is thus helping to determine if the session went well and if the elder is achieving the desired benefits from the activity. Revisions can be made based on the results of evaluation.

As the activity is completed, the leader should consider the following types of questions: Was the activity enjoyable? Was the activity too difficult or too easy? Was the activity too long for the allotted time? Does the elder wish to repeat the activity? Were the materials and supplies required for the activity adequate? What related activities may be attempted? What significant progress or behavior occurred during the activity?

Occasionally, the leader may be asked to summarize evaluation comments and report to the program coordinator. This might occur, for example, if problems were frequently encountered during activity time. The primary purpose of evaluation, however, is to help the leader learn how to make activity time as enjoyable and beneficial as possible.

UTILIZING THE ACTIVITY PLAN FORMAT

The activity session should follow the structure outlined in the activity plan format given below:

UNIT NAME:

ACTIVITY NAME:

PURPOSE OF ACTIVITY:

DESCRIPTION OF ACTIVITY:

BENEFITS OF ACTIVITY:

BEFORE THE SESSION:

>   Things to do

>   Things to take

WHAT TO DO DURING THE SESSION:

>   Greeting and opening chat; pay attention to any immediate needs.

>   Complete any unfinished business from previous session.

>   Explain the session's activities.

>   Do activities.

>   Session wrap-up; enjoy a snack if desired.

ENDING THE SESSION:

   Share the basket.

   Talk about and confirm next session.

AFTER THE SESSION:

   Write up comments.

IDEAS FOR MODIFYING THE ACTIVITY:

TIPS FOR SAFETY:

The activity plan begins with basic background information for the leader; it is important to be familiar with this basic information. The section "Before the Session" provides information regarding what the leader will need to do in preparation for the session. This section includes a listing of specific supplies and materials needed for the activity. In the third section, step-by-step instructions for conducting the activity are provided. Lastly, the activity plan includes ideas for modifying the session to meet certain needs of the elder and tips for safety.

Each session begins with a review of the activity conducted in the previous period and concludes with a preview of what will occur during the next session. This structure will assist in maintaining continuity and is particularly helpful if problems with short-term memory are present.

It is important for the leader to take time during the beginning of each session to note the present condition of the elder. Some days will not be good days. When this occurs, do not attempt to force the planned activity, as this will prove counterproductive. It is best to reschedule the activity or conduct it during the next regularly scheduled time. Noting the present condition of the elder also provides an opportunity to detect special problems and concerns, which may be referred by the sponsoring agency to other service providers such as visiting nurses, homemaker-health aides, etc.

Providing a time to share a snack is a special feature of the activity plan. This provides a good opportunity for social interaction. It also provides an opportunity for the elder to experience a feeling of responsibility and self-worth by preparing something for the session. Snacks should be simple and healthful. The leader should be familiar with any dietary restrictions indicated for the senior. The option to delete snack time can be chosen if desired. Having a banana or apple in a tote basket when going to a session ensures the opportunity for a snack, should the elder be unprepared.

Another optional feature of the activity plan is "sharing the basket." To "share the basket," the leader must work with two frail elderly persons or work in partnership with another leader. When working with each elder, the leaders ask if there is something of interest the elder would like the leaders to take and share with another person. The leaders then place the items in their tote baskets and listen to stories or information about the items. During the week, the leaders meet and exchange items and stories. In their next session with their elders, the leaders show the items and repeat the stories. On subsequent sessions, each leader will return a shared item, explain an item from the other elder, and collect a new item of significance to share in return. In this way, the leaders serve as a means of communication between two people, which may develop further through telephoning, letter writing, and possibly visiting. The types of items to be shared will vary. They might include pictures, postcards, souvenirs, edible items, craft items, stories, favorite sayings, jokes, trivia questions, etc. Do not take items of great worth! The possibility of misplacing an item is always a factor to consider.

At the end of each session, preferably after the session, the leader should record any significant progress or behavior that occurred during the activity. The leader should also note particular concerns or impressions. These written comments will be helpful in preparing to work with the elder each week and may also be shared with the program coordinator, if appropriate.

LEADERSHIP METHODS IN MOTIVATION*

Motivation is something that comes from within. "Motivating an individual to participate" really means stimulating a person's own motivation to seek involvement and self-direction.

Many elders will be self-motivated to participate in activities. Others, however, will only go through the motions or will not participate at all. While the senior's desire should be respected as much as possible, an attempt should be made to stimulate interest when nonacceptance threatens overall well-being.

There are two basic ways to stimulate an individual's own motivation. One is by the nature of the activity itself. Certain activities are by nature attractive and make the individual want to participate. In cases of reluctance to participate, time should be taken to determine which activities are attractive to the elder. The second method centers on coaxing participation. In some cases, it is necessary to get the senior involved at least to the extent that certain aspects of the

*Portions adapted from U.S. Department of Health, Education and Welfare. Activities coordinator's guide. HE22.208; L85. Washington, DC: U.S. Government Printing Office, 1978, pp. 22-24.

activity stimulate interests, resulting in motivation. Three approaches to coaxing are discussed below.

Involve the elder in many types of activities in the hope that one of them--or an aspect of one of them--will result in motivation. This approach may be likened to "sampling," whereby a person is exposed to a variety of activities and individual preferences are noted.

Present activities that are a direct reflection of the elder's interests and/or needs. For example, Mr. Doe has a need for social interaction and has expressed an interest in reading. Thus, the leader might suggest that Mr. Doe join in a discussion concerning a book of mutual interest.

Determine which aspects of a particular activity interest the elder so that activities containing these characteristics may be planned. For example, Mrs. Doe loves to reminisce and prefers activities with practical results. Thus, she might be motivated to make folk toys. This activity would allow for reminiscing and result in a product that could be displayed, given as a gift, or sold at a craft show.

Other suggestions that may help to ensure successful participation are listed below:

Try to put the elder at ease; create an accepting and supportive environment.

Take extra time to talk about needs, interests, and abilities.

Explain the program and encourage questions.

In the beginning, select activities that are most likely to succeed.

Make the elder feel as if participation is appreciated by the leader.

Give credit when it is due, but avoid flattery. A compliment on something that obviously did not turn out well can be belittling; but recognition of progress, however slight, is rewarding.

It may be necessary to allow the elder just to be a spectator in the beginning; this approach may stimulate the interest and encourage future participation.

Recognize the importance of timing. Everyone travels at an individual pace and readiness for involvement will differ. Someone who has been inactive for a number of years will require much nurturing. Move slowly in directing interests and realize that participation may occur during one session and not during the next.

Plan to spend more time during the "paying attention to immediate needs" section of the activities plan. Additional time spent listening and recognizing feelings may be needed before attempting the activity. In these cases, going immediately into an activity may hinder more than help the situation.

Recognize that some days just will not be good days, and efforts to conduct the activity will not be successful. In this situation, it is probably best to "just visit," perhaps ending the session early, to reschedule for another time during the week or to conduct the activity plan during the next regularly scheduled time.

BARRIERS TO EFFECTIVE COMMUNICATION*

Individuals are dependent on the ability to make their thoughts, feelings, and needs known to others. Effective communication is the result of those efforts. Communication is the sending and receiving of messages. The fact that a message was sent does not guarantee that it was received or understood.

For effective communication to be possible between any two persons, one must be aware of the conditions that may cause barriers to effective communication.

Conversation may be difficult if you are guilty of:	How to avoid these communication barriers
No eye contact	Look at the elder.
Cutting off elder	Allow the elder to finish.
Stereotyping	Don't allow appearances, body language, or what is said to turn you off.
Bypassing	Respond to what the elder has said before interjecting your thoughts.
Knowing it all	Allow yourself to learn from the elder. You may not have all the answers.
Inferring	Don't assume you know what the elder has to say. Don't finish the sentence.
Mind wandering	Give your attention.

*From Judith S. Justad, Executive Director, St. Paul YWCA, St. Paul, MN. Barriers to effective communication, unpublished material, 1983. Used by permission.

Defensiveness	Check out the other's intention before forming your opinion.
Hidden agenda	Help to clarify what the elder wishes to discuss so that you are both talking about the same issue.
Disinterest in needs	Listen for needs even though you also have needs to be met.
Put-down	Let the elder know that you will listen in a nonjudgmental manner.

If the leader has a communication problem during an activity, determine if any of these barriers exist.

SPECIAL SITUATIONS

During activity sessions, situations that merit special concern or consideration may occur. The elder might make a request which is unfamiliar to the leader. For example, the elder might ask the leader to assist with some specific medication or medical procedure. To prepare for these and other possible situations, be thoroughly familiar with the procedures specified by the sponsoring agency. Reviewing these procedures should be part of the initial training session and ongoing leader support meetings, as needed.

It is recommended that as persons are identified to receive the program, appropriate contacts in case of emergency are determined; this might be a relative, neighbor, visiting nurse, landlord. In addition, the sponsoring agency should have a telephone number and contact person available to the leader in special situations. In certain cases, it may be best to recommend that an activity session be held only during the operating hours of the agency so that a contact can be quickly made. The leader should write down this information and keep it in a convenient and accessible place. For example, the leader could record the information on an index card and carry it in a wallet, purse, or tote bag. Or this information could be kept in the elder's telephone book.

The emergency 911, if available, should be called only if it is an obvious emergency. This and other numbers of people to be called in special situations should be readily available. The leader should recognize personal limitations in dealing with special situations and should not attempt to overstep them.

Another situation of concern occurs when the elder attempts to extend the session. Ending an activity is sometimes difficult, a situation that needs special emphasis. Perhaps the best way to avoid a difficult ending to a session is prevention. The following ideas are presented as ways to help control the time spent during a session.

Closely follow the activity plan format, beginning with "What to do during the session."

As the activities are explained, briefly summarize what will occur during the session, clarifying expectations and briefly reviewing the structure of the activity; state the time available for the session.

As the ending time draws near, begin expressing enjoyment and appreciation and make references to the next session; perhaps verbally note the current time. For example, "This has been an enjoyable session and I appreciate your company and participation. It's three o'clock, however, and it's time for me to leave until our next meeting."

Use nonverbal exit clues such as partly or completely rising from a chair, lessening eye contact, glancing at the clock or one's watch, shaking the elder's hand, etc.

If the session time consistently runs longer than desired, the following ideas may be of assistance.

Plan to conduct a portion of "Doing Activities" only. Do not attempt to finish the entire activity in one session.

Provide a cheerful but firm reminder regarding the desired length of time of the session; seek a mutual agreement on the desired time limit. For example, in a lighthearted manner, state, "We have not been doing too well on ending our sessions on time! It's important for me to keep to about one hour in length, and I think that's best for you, too. Don't you agree?" In some situations, this reminder might need to be given at the beginning of each session.

Begin ending the session after 40 to 45 minutes by giving a verbal signal that the time is almost up. For example, "Mary, I have just noticed that we have about 10 minutes left. Let's review what we've done today and what we'll cover during the next session."

If the senior continues to discuss new topics, respond, "I can see you still have some things you'd like to talk about, yet we don't have time today. Let's see when our next session is."

Plan the session before a regularly scheduled activity. For example, one senior living in a retirement center regularly ate supper with the other residents at 5:30 p.m. Thus, the leader scheduled the sessions for 4:00 p.m., assuring that it would end within 1½ hours.

The leader should demonstrate by words and actions the intention to leave. That is, when the leader says it is time to leave and stands to leave, he/she should then leave! The elder will better understand

the time limits if the leader consistently leaves at the designated
time. If the leader states an intention to leave and then stays for
an additional length of time, the signals will be confusing and lead
to a belief that the leader really does have more time available.

Ending the session at the designated time does not mean rejection.
In fact, sticking to the time limits will prove of greater benefit
for both. End the session on an upbeat, positive note, making reference
to the next one. In time, the elder will understand and appreciate
the time limit and will realize that the leader will come again at
the next designated time.

Special situations involving problem behavior are occasionally found
when working with an elder who has been without social contact for
years. Such situations may be easier to manage if the leader seeks
help from appropriate resource personnel to determine the most effective
methods of dealing with extreme or long-term problem behavior. The
following are general examples of problem behaviors. Basic leadership
suggestions for solving them are then given (Des Moines Area Community
College, 1983).

Depression

Show sincere interest, but don't be overly cheerful or superficial.
Give simple directions.
Do not force the elder to make too many decisions.
Watch for signs of fatigue.

Withdrawal

Present directions in a simple, direct manner.
Be friendly and accepting.
Do not go along with an elder's fantasy world, but do not try
  to argue him or her out of it.
Be alert for unusual behavior.

Anxiety

Provide simple activities that are easily mastered.
Try to redirect excessive talk about physical symptoms.
Be patient and supportive in a low-key manner.

Suspiciousness

Be completely honest. Keep physical contact to a minimum.
Be consistent, friendly, but not superficial.
Do not act secretive--be matter-of-fact.
Accept aggressive, hostile, or aloof behavior as a symptom of
  the problem; do not take it personally. Try to redirect this
  behavior.
Call in advance of visit.

Give your name at the door, i.e., "Wilma, it's Donna. I've come
  to visit."
Don't attempt to "share the basket" using actual items if the
  elder is concerned about parting with possessions for the week.
  Use sayings, stories, jokes, etc., instead.

Mental confusion

Use activities that help the elder stay in contact with reality,
  reminding them of the date and time.
Avoid frustrating activities.
Be patient and reassuring in manner.

CONFIDENTIALITY

At times during the program, the leader will see, hear, write, or
read confidential information. Confidential information is any
communication to, or observation by, the leader which is not clearly
intended to be shared with another person. Exceptions could be another
person who is directly involved in providing services to the elder
or the program coordinator.

The elder may determine or control the nature of the information he/she
wishes to disclose. If the elder chooses not to answer questions
that the leader feels are important to conducting a safe and successful
session, the leader should then contact the program coordinator for
assistance. The leader should not collect any personal information
that is clearly not necessary for the program.

Examples of confidential information include:

Information given in confidence by the elder in the course of
receiving the program activities.

Information that is given in confidence by family, friends,
neighbors, etc.

Any opinion, summary, or instruction concerning the elder given
by sponsoring agency personnel in the course of the program.

Personal information which, if told to others, could possibly
be detrimental to the best interests of the elder.

REFERENCES AND RESOURCES

Austin, D. R. Therapeutic recreation, processes and techniques.
New York: John Wiley and Sons, 1982.

Austin, D. R., & Powell, L. G. Resource guide: College instruction in recreation for individuals with handicapping conditions. Bloomington, IN: Indiana University, 1980.

Black, K. Short-term counseling, a humanistic approach for the helping professions. Reading, MA: Addison-Wesley Publishing Company, 1983.

Bullock, C. C., Wohl, R. E., Webeck, T. E., & Crawford, A. M. Leisure is for everyone: Resource and training manual. Chapel Hill, NC: Curriculum in Recreation Administration, University of North Carolina at Chapel Hill, 1982.

Cormier, S. L., Cormier, W. H., & Weisser, R. J. Interviewing and helping skills for health professionals. Belmont, CA: Wadsworth, Inc., 1984.

Des Moines Area Community College. Activity director workshop manual. Estherville, IA: Iowa Lakes Community College, 1983.

Hamill, C. M., & Oliver, R. C. Therapeutic activities for the handicapped elderly. Rockville, MD: Aspens Systems Corporation, 1980.

Justad, Judith S., Executive Director, St. Paul YWCA, St. Paul, MN. Barriers to effective communication. Unpublished material, 1983.

Kraus, R. Therapeutic recreation service: Principles and practices (3d ed.). Philadelphia: Saunders College Publishing, 1981.

Kraus, R. G., Carpenter, G., & Bates, B. J. Recreation leadership and supervision. Philadelphia: Saunders College Publishing, 1981.

Moran, J. M. Leisure activities for the mature adult. Minneapolis, MN: Burgess Publishing, 1980.

O'Morrow, G. S. Therapeutic recreation: A helping profession (2nd ed.). Reston, VA: Reston Publishing, 1980, p. 139.

Peterson, C. A., & Gunn, S. L. Therapeutic recreation program design (2nd ed.). Englewood Cliffs, NJ: Prentice-Hall, 1984.

Purtilo, R. The allied health professional and the patient. Philadelphia: W. B. Saunders, 1973.

Russell, R. V. Leadership in recreation. St. Louis: Time Mirror/Mosby College Publishing, 1986.

Shivers, J. S., & Fait, H. F. Special recreational services: Therapeutic and adapted. Philadelphia: Lea & Febiger, 1985.

Stein, T. A., & Sessoms, H. D. Recreation and special populations (2nd ed.). Boston: Holbrook Press, 1977.

U.S. Department of Health, Education and Welfare. <u>Activities coordinator's guide</u>. HE22.208; L85. Washington, DC: U.S. Government Printing Office, 1978.

Wehman, P., & Schleien, S. <u>Leisure programs for handicapped persons</u>. Baltimore: University Park Press, 1981.

CHAPTER 4

Coordinating the Program

At a time when Mother Teresa was in Australia setting up her mission, she was walking in the most undesirable of places and stepped into the horribly dirty and dusty room of an old man that all the people walking with her had passed by. In the midst of all the dirt was a dusty, but very beautiful ornate lamp. The first thing Mother Teresa asked the old man was why he didn't have the lamp turned on. The old man just looked at her and replied: "For whom? No one comes to see me. I don't need the lamp." Mother Teresa asked him if one of her sisters came to visit would he then agree to turn the lamp on. The old man answered, "Only if I hear a human voice." It was many months later, the old man sent Mother Teresa a message: "Tell my friend that the lamp she lit in my life is still burning."

--Robert Serrou

Successful implementation of the program requires coordination between each of the elements unique to this program. These elements are discussed below.

1. A population that is receptive to receiving a program

The individuals to be served by the leaders in the program will be primarily older adults who have one or more physical, emotional, intellectual, or social limitation, and are in need of assistance to achieve and maintain their level of independent living. These people may not live alone; however, they may be in need of social interaction and cannot leave the home or institution without assistance.

2. People willing to be trained to carry out the program

The persons carrying out the program should be able to relate to older people on a one-to-one basis in a home or institutional setting and be willing to work with the program coordinator. The leaders should be willing to accept support or supervision from the coordinator when needed and give feedback and support to other leaders. They should be punctual, dependable, and respectful of the confidential nature of the leader-elder relationship.

3. **An organization that can provide appropriate support to the program and leaders**

Examples of existing organizations that provide access to the three elements are Retired Senior Volunteer Programs having a friendly visiting component, multipurpose senior centers, churches with an educational staff and a program for visiting home-centered members, and community leisure service centers. Nursing homes with activity coordinators and aids, or visiting nurses organizations with homemaker health aides would also provide a suitable structure for carrying out the program. Senior companions, youth organizations, and university students and instructors desiring intergenerational activities are other potential structures that might utilize the materials.

A strong supporting agency must make a commitment to the program. This includes allotting manpower, money, and time. The leaders will need support in the form of adequate health and safety protection. Leadership training will be an agency responsibility as well as providing space for training sessions and support meetings.

In addition, the organization must be able to relate effectively to a needy elderly population. The selection of a qualified program coordinator will contribute greatly to establishing an effective relationship between the sponsoring agency and the participant.

Finally, there are some costs associated with the program. The agency may be able to serve as the source of these funds. If there are no internal financial resources, the agency or organization can serve as the dispersing (fiscal) agent for the program, using funds generated from external sources. Typical program expenses include the following:

Salary of the program coordinator

Purchase of program training and activity books

Cost of refreshments and/or lunch during training, and recognition banquet or social gathering at the end of each unit or year

Advertising and other costs related to disseminating information about the program

Transportation and meal reimbursement for leaders, when applicable

STEPS TO IMPLEMENT THE PROGRAM

Although agency differences will exist, the following steps are suggested as guidelines for implementing the program:

1. Identify the need for the program.

2. Locate a suitable existing agency to implement the program.

3. Identify a staff member to coordinate the program.

4. Advertise the program through existing channels, i.e., newspapers, senior newsletters, church bulletins, flyers or placemats at congregate meal sites, college catalogs.

5. Begin establishing a leader pool.

6. Ask for referrals of frail elderly from appropriate human service agencies.

7. Interview and enroll elders before delivery of the program, specifying the nature and duration of the program.

8. Organize and schedule the training program and contact community resource persons to contribute.

9. The program coordinator should conduct several activity plans with an elder to better understand the activity plan design and the experiences of delivering one-on-one activities.

10. Establish a resource library for the leaders, including many of the things needed when conducting sessions. Each item should be cataloged according to the unit or units in which it will be used.

11. Conduct, if needed, a funding drive to purchase tote baskets for leaders to use, money for a recognition banquet, and other out-of-pocket expenses as desired.

12. Conduct the training program.

13. Match leaders and elders.

14. Schedule meeting times when leaders can meet as a group for support, guidance, and encouragement.

15. Begin the program.

16. Talk to each leader at the meetings or by phone to follow up on needs and problems.

17. Maintain records of the participants in the program, indicating the interests of elder and leader, units delivered, and special concerns.

18. Maintain records of hours leaders have served.

19. Resolve problems arising among the leader, the elder, and the agency.

20. Conduct leader recognition activities as desired.

21. Repeat steps 12 to 14 after every unit or when needed.

The length of time it takes to implement these steps will vary from setting to setting. Recruiting efforts will be influenced by the types of agencies or organizations that are present in a community and their level of effectiveness. One important consideration in developing the time line should be training the leaders before interest lags. Keep in mind that both leader and elder, having committed themselves, are eager to begin the sessions.

Another important consideration is the material to be included in the training program. (Refer to Appendix B.) A minimum of 8 hours is recommended to cover the subject matter adequately. Role-playing and hands-on experience with the materials are vital aspects of training. The training schedule should allow for adequate time to elapse between meetings so that leaders can practice or actually conduct a session with an elder, returning to share that experience with the group.

Once training is completed and sessions are underway, the coordinator provides ongoing support to the leaders by being available to answer questions and help solve problems associated with the delivery of sessions. Depending on the needs of the group, regular support meetings may be scheduled to allow for group interaction and sharing of information and support. Telephone contact on a regular basis is helpful when meetings are impossible; however, group meetings help to develop a feeling of togetherness. Structuring meetings around specific activities from the activity plans is an effective way of bolstering confidence. Leaders may also use this time to contribute their own adaptations of the activities, thereby accomplishing one of the goals of the program, i.e., using these materials as a springboard for creating one's own activity plans.

Finally, the coordinator plans a recognition banquet or other social gathering at the end of the unit. In most cases leaders invite elders, thereby adding special meaning to the culmination of one unit by bringing the elder to a social function to meet others who have been involved with the same program.

RECRUITING AND ENROLLING LEADERS

The leader is the person who carries the program to the elder and brings the concept to life. For both, the quality of the experience will depend to a large extent on the skills of the coordinator who works to recruit, train, and motivate the leaders.

Recruiting volunteers will be an important consideration for some agencies. others will already have a pool of names from which to draw leaders. For those agencies who must recruit new names or rebuild existing files, the following suggestions are offered:

Make use of existing channels to advertise, i.e., senior newsletters, newspapers, church bulletins, radio, public service television announcements.

Speak at meetings frequented by older people.

Make presentations to community volunteer organizations.

Contact inactive volunteers.

Make presentations to agencies that provide home services to the elderly, such as Meals-On-Wheels, homemaker health aides, and visiting nurses.

Once advertising has begun and potential leaders express interest, the coordinator may want to schedule an informational meeting of 45 to 60 minutes and invite interested persons. Make the meeting less threatening by advertising it as a "Coffee and Information Hour," a chance to meet other potential leaders and find out more about the program.

At this meeting, the coordinator can present a description of the program and a time line for training and beginning the sessions. Stress that training is participation-oriented, enjoyable, and nonthreatening. Stress also that training will provide the skills and practice in how to interact with frail, home-centered elderly persons.

The meeting will enable the coordinator to interview and enroll new leaders. The sponsoring organization may have established enrollment procedures and forms. If not, the organization will need to develop appropriate procedures and forms. Basic information, such as address, phone, emergency contact, etc., should be recorded, as well as related information, such as special needs (time constraints, transportation constraints, etc.), skills and interests, and previous experience. Information provided will be helpful in matching leaders and elders.

Commitment to the program, in terms of hours, would be approximately 8 hours for the training program, 1 hour per week for up to 9 sessions, 30 minutes preparation time for each session, and an optional 60 minutes for weekly (or bi-monthly) meetings with other leaders to exchange information and support.

RECRUITING AND ENROLLING ELDERS

Locating recipients for the program might be difficult without the cooperation of existing service providers and other community organizations. With their help and with the help of members of the community-at-large, it will be possible to form a pool of elderly people who receive some form of social service as well as some who do not receive assistance and are therefore not on agency lists. Those in the latter group are accessible only through friends and/or relatives who come in contact with the program through one of the means of advertising discussed above in recruitment of leaders.

Once potential recipients have been identified, the coordinator arranges to visit each person to interview and enroll them. Many home-centered people are wary of strangers, and some are deluged with more calls and information than they can comfortably handle. It is therefore helpful when contacting the home-centered elderly person to refer to the name of a person or agency familiar to him or her. Information should be well organized and concise, and presented slowly. A telephone call before a scheduled visit helps the elder prepare to answer the door--which requires real effort for many.

During the first visit between coordinator and elder, the interview information may be recorded on a form and the elder's signature obtained. Basic information such as address, phone, emergency contact, etc., should be recorded as well as information pertaining to special concerns and precautions, interests and skills, and social services currently receiving.

MATCHING LEADERS AND ELDERS

The information recorded during the interview will be useful to the coordinator when matching leader and elder. Consideration should be given to the personalities and interests of the potential pairs as well as their proximity to one another. As much as possible, leaders should be assigned an elder in their own neighborhoods. The session times are arranged between the leader and the elder. Even after matching is completed, both parties have the right to request a change; however, at the end of the unit, the two are not expected to be matched for subsequent units.

MOTIVATING AND RETAINING LEADERS

Leaders are naturally motivated and interested, but it is the role of the coordinator to further develop and nurture that motivation and interest. Visiting programs have been particularly susceptible to "burnout." This program tries to combat burnout; the delivery system, activity materials, training, and unit cycles, all support the nurturing of both leader and elder. Service to an elder can continue by rotating assignments after every unit. This also provides the opportunity for a leader to take a break, by opting to not work for the next unit cycle.

Two of the best motivators for leaders are recognizing their accomplishments and providing opportunities for self-improvement.

Aspects of the program that enhance self-worth in leaders are:

1. Acquisition of new leadership skills in an enjoyable, nonthreatening manner.

2. A certificate of training given to each leader at the completion of the training (optional).

3. A tote basket given to each leader who completes the training (optional).

4. Meetings with other leaders to exchange ideas, share questions and answers, and offer mutual support.

5. A recognition banquet or social gathering at the end of each unit or at the completion of several units.

Recognition of leaders is an ongoing process; each situation requires a slightly different approach. Some of the most valuable resources are the leaders themselves. Peer interest and support can come about through the scheduled meetings of leaders. Weekly meetings may be desired when the program is new and later taper off to twice a month. These meetings are, however, important to maintenance of the program over a long period of time.

During the early stages of recruiting and training, the coordinator must exercise judgment about the commitment and motivations of individual leaders. If the leader still seems unable to perform as desired, it is the responsibility of the coordinator to recommend, as firmly and kindly as possible, an alternate assignment. Stress appreciation for efforts made and offer an opportunity to try again sometime later.

DEVELOPING A RESOURCE LIBRARY

Resources are another form of support for the leader as well as for
the program. For this reason, formation of a resource library is
recommended. Although the program materials are designed to make
use only of easily found supplies, there are a few that might require
cooperative effort. Pooling resources and providing storage for them
in some accessible space will not only provide the leader with the
necessary supplies but also the opportunity to meet with the other
leaders. One person may wish to serve as the librarian, organizing
the materials according to the units in which they are used. Appendix
B contains an equipment list itemizing the materials needed to carry
out each activity unit.

Another kind of resource to add to this library is a list of individuals
with skills to offer. Everyone could contribute to this file, which
would contain the names, addresses, phone numbers, and special skills
of individuals who might be willing to contribute to the program in
some way. A file of organizations offering specific services, or
hobby groups, also would be useful information. An important facet
of the program, enhanced by a resource file, is helping to bring the
elder into contact with community services and providing contact with
others who share similar interests. The leader can use the resource
file as a vital link in the process of reintegrating the elder with
the community.

REFERENCES AND RESOURCES

Crandall, R. C. Gerontology: A behavioral science approach. Reading,
MA: Addison-Wesley Publishing Company, 1980.

Cutler, S. J. Aging and voluntary association participation. Journal
of Gerontology 32(4): 470-479, 1980.

Hale, G. (Ed.). Source book for the disabled. New York: Bantam
Books, 1979.

Labanowich, S., Andrews, N., & Pollock, J. Recreation for the
home-bound aging. Lexington, KY: Department of Health, Physical
Education and Recreation, University of Kentucky, 1978.

Leiter, M. M. Shaping the body politic: Legislative training for
the physical educator. American Alliance of Health, Physical Education,
Recreation and Dance, 1900 Association Drive, Reston, VA 22091.

Peralta, V. Informal helping resources: Innovative use and support
for senior centers. In Working with the at-risk older person.
Washington, DC: National Council on the Aging, 1981.

Retired Senior Volunteer Program. Operation handbook 4405.92, August 15, 1983, Washington, DC.

Senior Companion Program. Operations handbook 4405.91, August 15, 1983, Washington, DC.

Serrou, R. Teresa of Calcutta, p. 78. New York: McGraw-Hill, 1980.

Stone, J. Second careers volunteer program. New York: Mayor's Voluntary Action Center, 1980.

Trela, J. E. Social class and association memberships: An analysis of age-guarded and nonage-guarded voluntary participation. Journal of Gerontology 31(2): 198-203, 1976.

Trent, B. (Ed.). A practical guide to recruiting, training, and evaluating volunteers in the recreation center. Clemson, SC: Clemson University, Extension Report RPA 1981/82-7.

U.S. Department of the Interior. Volunteer handbook. Washington, DC: Heritage Conservation and Recreation Service, 1978.

_____. Scrounging. Washington, DC: Heritage Conservation and Recreation Service, 1980.

PART II
Activities

CHAPTER 5

Special Features of the Program

STARTING A UNIT

Gathering and interpreting information about the elder helps the leader to make decisions when starting a recreation unit. Assessment is time devoted to the measurement or evaluation of a person's current or perceived future status. This can occur in a formal situation such as a student completing an exam, or informally as when the family sits around the dinner table discussing whether the dog or cat is sick and needs a trip to the veterinarian. Administering and interpreting formal assessments, such as an electrocardiogram or an IQ test, require special training. Informal assessments can be done by anyone; however, it is difficult to compare the results with other information.

Before engaging in a series of planned recreation activities, some time should be spent assessing a person's current condition. This is even more important when the person is very old and/or frail. Without assessing condition, a leader risks failure in meeting the intended results of the unit and will not know how best to meet the needs of the elder. Interpreting the assessment results will help the leader to get acquainted in a very short time. In addition, areas of concern or deficiency may be found. The leader can then inform the program coordinator about the problem and the coordinator can follow up by contacting a social service program. The leader has then helped to bring services other than recreation into the elder's life.

The leader needs to know the elder's current condition in eyesight and hearing. These physical factors are used in every unit. Should a unit require modification, it is best if the leader can anticipate the changes needed.

Since declines in performing physical tasks are sometimes an embarrassment to an older person, it is best to use informal techniques to identify current conditions. In addition, eyesight and hearing cannot be expected to change because of these program activities. The primary purpose for assessing these factors is to anticipate needed adaptations in activities. As an example of how an informal assessment can help an activity succeed, two hypothetical situations are presented below.

In one instance, the leader assesses the elder's visual abilities during the first session by informally looking over the list of unit names and descriptions, found on pages xi and xiii. The elder and leader are sitting next to one another on a couch, in good lighting, with the elder holding the list. The leader reads the name and description of a unit and then asks if there is another of interest to read. If the elder asks for a unit by name, the leader knows he/she can read the print. After reading the unit description, the leader asks the elder if he/she would like to read the description of a particular unit. If the description is read, more is learned about the ability to see and read print. If the elder declines, the leader continues to read descriptions.

In a second situation, the leader has not previously assessed the elder's ability to read the print before attempting to complete the Literature Unit. During a session some printed material is handed to the elder. The leader asks the elder to read information from the material. Embarrassment results because the elder can't read the print. Rejection of the activity occurs, and the elder does not want to continue. Restarting the session using a different approach isn't possible now that the elder is defensive.

In the first situation, the elder always had a way to gracefully decline reading aloud. Reading was an option and was led into slowly. In the second situation, the elder was thrust headfirst into a reading task. By the time it became obvious that reading was impossible, the activity was in progress and came to an uncomfortable halt. There was no alternative except to admit failure.

It will be obvious during the first session if the elder has difficulty hearing. Other subtle clues are the presence of a telephone, record player, or radio. The leader can also simply ask if the elder enjoys listening to the radio.

The leader can purposely talk in different ways to see if the conversation is followed. For instance, turn away from the elder momentarily and say something. If the elder can still relate to what was said, hearing ability should be sufficient for the program activities without modification.

As described above, sight and reading skills can be assessed by asking the elder to read the unit descriptions. A refusal to do so does not necessarily indicate a visual impairment; however, it does show a reluctance to join in activities that require reading.

ASSESSING RECREATION INTERESTS

Determining the elder's recreation interests will give the leader an idea of which activities the elder is curious about, already involved in, "likes," is skilled at, etc. The areas surveyed in the following checklist are useful to the leader in determining activities in which the elder is interested, thus indicating the recreation unit the elder might enjoy. Names in parentheses reflect the units containing activities similar to the survey item.

RECREATION INTEREST SURVEY

CRAFTS

( )   DRAWING/PAINTING/SCULPTURE......................(Crafts, Hobbies)
( )   CERAMICS/POTTERY...(Crafts)
( )   LEATHERWORK..(Crafts)
( )   WEAVING..(Crafts)
( )   WOODWORKING..(Crafts)
( )   JEWELRY MAKING...(Crafts)
( )   MODEL BUILDING..(Crafts)
( )   FLOWER ARRANGING..(Hobbies)
( )   KNITTING/CROCHETING/NEEDLEWORK...........................(Crafts)
( )   QUILTING/SEWING...(Crafts)
( )   OTHER

SPORTS

( )   SWIMMING...(Exercise)
( )   CROQUET/SHUFFLEBOARD......................................(Games)
( )   BICYCLING..(Exercise)
( )   EXERCISING...(Exercise)
( )   WALKING/JOGGING..(Exercise)
( )   TENNIS...(Exercise)
( )   GOLF...(Exercise)
( )   BOWLING..(Exercise, Games)
( )   DANCING--Square, Social, Ballroom......................(Exercise)
( )   HORSESHOES.........................(Games, Remembering the Past)
( )   BILLIARDS/POOL...(Games)
( )   OTHER

LITERARY

( )   WRITING POETRY OR STORES.......(Literature, Remembering the Past)
( )   LETTER WRITING......................................(Literature)
( )   READING...............Hobbies, Literature, Remembering the Past)
( )   OTHER

TABLE GAMES

( )   CHESS..(Games)
( )   CHECKERS/DOMINOES..(Games)
( )   CARDS--Bridge, Cribbage, Poker, Hearts....................(Games)
( )   BINGO...(Games, Literature)
( )   PUZZLES--Crossword/Jigsaw.......................(Games, Hobbies)
( )   OTHER

MUSIC

( )   LISTENING....................................(Literature, Hobbies)
( )   PLAYING MUSICAL INSTRUMENT............................(Hobbies)
( )   OTHER

INTELLECTUAL PURSUITS

( )   DISCUSSION GROUPS..............(Remembering the Past, Literature)
( )   ATTEND LECTURES.......................................(Hobbies)
( )   VISIT MUSEUMS, LIBRARIES, CULTURAL CENTERS.....................
       ....(Crafts, Literature, Hobbies)
( )   OTHER

SPECTATOR APPRECIATION

( )   MOVIES........................(Remembering the Past, Literature)
( )   SIGHTSEEING/TRAVEL/TRAVELOGUES..............(Hobbies, Literature)
( )   SPORTS.......................................(Exercise, Games)
( )   OTHER

MISCELLANEOUS

( )   GARDENING/HOUSEPLANTS.........................(Hobbies, Exercise)
( )   PHOTOGRAPHY...(Hobbies)
( )   PETS.......................................(Remembering the Past)
( )   COLLECTING THINGS.................(Hobbies, Remembering the Past)
( )   DIETING/NUTRITION....................................(Exercise)
( )   BIRD WATCHING...(Hobbies)
( )   OTHER

CLUBS AND ORGANIZATIONS

( )   POLITICAL.....................(Literature, Remembering the Past)
( )   CHURCH..........(Remembering the Past, Crafts, Games, Literature)
( )   UNIONS.......................................(Remembering the Past)
( )   PROFESSIONAL CLUBS...............(Hobbies, Remembering the Past)
( )   FRATERNITIES/SORORITIES..................(Remembering the Past)

To administer the Recreation Interest Survey, the leader simply reads
the recreation activity examples under each category and asks the
elder if he/she is currently interested in, or "likes," the activity;
if yes, the leader places a check by that activity. If desired, the

leader may further explore the elder's past participation in the activity and future intentions about the activity. The leader should write down this additional information about each activity on the survey checklist. Other recreation activities not included on the checklist should be added if they are mentioned by the elder. The leader may choose to give the elder a copy of the survey. Both would then complete their surveys while comparing results and discussing common interests.

Review the activities the elder has selected from the Recreation Interest Survey. Notice the names of the units included in this volume, and the activity of exercise from the Exercise Activities and the Elderly book are listed below. To score the survey(s), count the number of checked survey items for each particular unit, or for exercise. For instance, if the activities of LISTENING, DRAWING/PAINTING/SCULPTURE, and COLLECTING THINGS are checked on the survey, count three for the Hobbies Unit, one for the Remembering the Past Unit, one for the Crafts Unit, and one for the Literature Unit.

Examples from the survey:
( )   COLLECTING THINGS.................(Hobbies, Remembering the Past)
( )   DRAWING/PAINTING/SCULPTURE......................(Crafts, Hobbies)
( )   LISTENING...................................(Literature, Hobbies)

Units

Hobbies   √√√
Remembering the Past   √
Crafts   √
Literature   √
Games
Exercise

A quick look at the frequency of selection will show which units the elder might prefer. Read the description of the units receiving the highest scores. Discuss which units seem the most attractive, and choose one to utilize during the upcoming sessions. If the selection indicates an interest in exercise, the units in the Exercise Activities and the Elderly book are recommended.

Assessment must be kept in perspective. A person cannot be understood by marks on a score sheet. A clearer understanding of the elder will evolve as a unit progresses. The leader must be flexible; a formal assessment should not be forced if the elder does not want to participate. The recreation assessment should be utilized merely as a starting point, enjoyed for itself, with laughter and discussion along the way.

COMMUNITY RESOURCE REFERRAL

After seven sessions have been completed the leader and elder should be acquainted. This will be the appropriate time to spend one session on networking the elder into recreation activities in the community. In some situations, such a transition may be impossible; however, delivered services can be encouraged for even the most severely restricted.

An activity plan to help the leader structure this session can be found on pages 59 to 62. Resources specific to each community must be identified by the leader or program coordinator prior to this session. This activity plan is usable with any unit.

ENDING A UNIT

The last session in a unit serves two purposes. First, the leader can follow up on the community resource referral session. It is important to verify that contacts were made, and the elder and program directors are communicating. The second purpose is to allow the elder a chance to reflect on the unit and repeat any favorite activities.

No activity plan is included for this ninth session, as the direction and flow should come from the elder. As the leader finishes the "Community Resource Referral" session, ask the elder, "Mary, of the activities that we have done together over the past several weeks, which would you like to repeat next session?" The leader should be prepared for responses such as, "Oh! Why don't we visit next time?" or "I don't know, you decide." The leader may follow the "let's visit" suggestion with visiting, as this is a choice and decision expressed by the elder. In the case of the "don't know" response, the leader can try naming activities completed together, in hopes that the elder will select one.

Since it is not practical for the leader to carry all of the "things to take" items in the tote basket on this last visit, prepare for the visit by deciding the activity in advance as suggested above, then gather specific items as required. Remember, the elder may wish to repeat any of the previous sessions.

ACTIVITY UNITS

Each of the following units contains activity plans for six sessions. It is possible, however, that one activity plan may require more than one session to complete. In addition, not all activity plans per unit may be suitable for the elder. Selection of the units and corresponding activities will depend on the unique needs and interests of the elder.

Other activity units, of an exercise nature, can be found in the accompanying volume, Exercise Activities and the Elderly.

UNIT NAME: All Units

ACTIVITY PLAN 1: ASSESSING RECREATION INTERESTS

PURPOSE OF THE ACTIVITY: To learn the recreation interests of the elder and the leader. To provide an opportunity for the elder and the leader to get to know each other. To choose a unit to use for the remaining sessions.

DESCRIPTION OF ACTIVITY: The elder and leader will complete a recreation interest survey, either written or oral. After scoring the survey, they will read descriptions of the units receiving high scores.

BENEFITS OF ACTIVITY: This session provides some subjective information about the elder and the leader which can lead to conversations about personal interests. Information gained in this session will help the leader prepare for future sessions.

BEFORE THE SESSION:

    Things to do

Contact the elder to schedule the session time. Make a short personal visit as an introduction if the elder seems concerned or skeptical about the program.

Photocopy the Recreation Interest Survey and the Unit Descriptions from pages xii to xiii.

Things to take

Pencils with erasers
Clipboard or lapboard for writing
Recreation Interest Survey
Unit descriptions

WHAT TO DO DURING THE SESSION:

Greeting and opening chat; pay attention to any immediate needs.

This is the first meeting between the elder and leader. It may be
difficult to do a paper-and-pencil activity with the elder for a variety
of physical or mental reasons. The leader must be ready to adapt,
on the spot, to such situations. One of the most likely difficulties
is the elder's reluctance to do any activity beyond talking. A second
problem may result if the elder distrusts the paper-and-pencil approach
with a stranger. The leader may need to talk about the elder's
recreation interests informally and make the best effort possible
to match the elder's interests to the recreation activity units.
A reluctance to complete the Recreation Interest Survey may be an
indication that the elder is not ready for structured activity. In
such cases the Remembering the Past Unit can be useful, where the
elder and leader can discuss each session topic in a conversational
mode. The elder need not feel part of a structured program of
recreational activities.

Explain the session's activities.

Do activities.

The leader will ask the elder if he/she is currently interested in,
or "likes," each of the activities listed in the Recreation Interest
Survey and will record the elder's responses. The leader is also
encouraged to ask the elder if he/she enjoyed the activity in the
past, or is interested in future participation. The elder may prefer
to receive a copy of the survey and complete it independently. In
this situation, while the elder completes the written survey, the
leader can do likewise.

Session wrap-up; enjoy a snack if desired.

As this is the first session, the elder probably will not have prepared
a snack, or even realize it is a part of the program. The leader
may choose to take a snack to share at this time.

ENDING THE SESSION:

Write up comments.

Make notes about observations made during the session on the elder's sight, hearing, and use of hands. Any limitations that might affect participation can be noted for adaptations in unit activities.

IDEAS FOR MODIFYING THE SESSION: Assessment should not be forced if the elder does not want to participate. The conversation approach mentioned in the "Greeting and opening chat" section of this activity plan is an important adaptation. The leader may also choose to self-administer the Recreation Interest Survey and let the elder help. As the leader assesses his/her interests, the elder may be drawn into the conversation and activity.

TIPS FOR SAFETY: Make sure the lighting is adequate and the elder is comfortable.

UNIT NAME: All Units

ACTIVITY PLAN 8: COMMUNITY RESOURCE REFERRAL

PURPOSE OF ACTIVITY: To present the elder with knowledge about various community resources through which interests developed during the course of this unit may be continued, and the needs for instrumental support can be met.

DESCRIPTION OF ACTIVITY: The leader will describe various community resources for seniors. Some resources should pertain to the topic of this unit, others to the general well-being of the elder. The leader and elder will then discuss ways to continue an interest in the unit topic, specific resources the elder would like to contact, and a plan for how the elder can use these resources.

BENEFITS OF ACTIVITY: The leader identifies various community resources through which the elder can continue pursuing interests in the unit topic. Through this referral process the leader is helping the elder to discover ways to engage in the recreation activities without the help of the leader. This session helps to involve the elder in activities of the community to the greatest possible extent. Involvement in community activities is stressed, regardless of extent. This session also informs the elder that other services are available to help seniors meet nutritional, transportation, and health needs.

BEFORE THE SESSION:

   Things to do

During the time the leader and elder have been participating in the activities of this unit the leader has learned about the interests and needs of the elder. The leader is now ready to refer the elder to appropriate community resources through which interests can be pursued. To accomplish this the leader must spend some time prior to this session locating local community resources and gathering information about services and opportunities available to the elder. The leader and elder will determine which of the local community resources are appropriate to pursue. Community resources must be apropriate in light of the interests, needs, and limitations (health, transportation, finances) of the elder.

1. The leader makes a reference list of related community resources to leave with the elder. For example, an index card containing names of contact people and their phone numbers could be left by the telephone, tacked to a bulletin board, or inserted in a phone book. Listed below are examples of organizations, agencies, or personnel that may provide information to the leader.

    Park and recreation departments, districts, or commissions
    Senior centers
    YMCAs or YWCAs
    Churches and other service-oriented groups
    County extension offices
    Individuals from the community
    Merchants selling materials for various recreation needs
    Libraries--good sources for locating information pertaining to organizations, individuals, or related resources
    Chambers of Commerce
    Yellow pages in the phone book

2. To learn about services designed to help seniors in institutions or in their homes, the leader might contact the Area Agency on Aging. Listed below are examples of services to help provide instrumental support to such persons.

    Home-delivered meals
    Home health care
    Homemaker service
    Transportation assistance
    Legal aid
    Handyman chore service

    Things to take

Paper or index cards
Pencil
Resource materials (any pamphlets and brochures that are available)

WHAT TO DO DURING THE SESSION:

   Greeting and opening chat; pay attention to any immediate needs.

   Complete any unfinished business from previous session.

   Explain the session's activities.

   Do activities.

Discuss various community resources of interest to the elder by describing the type of service available from each resource and suggesting how this resource might be utilized. Assist the elder in selecting appropriate resources for future contact.

Once preferred resources have been selected, discuss how these might be contacted. On a piece of paper or index card, write the following information:

1. Name of the agency and/or individual resource person
2. Address and telephone number
3. Type of service
4. Various questions the elder would like to ask (such as questions about cost, transportation, mailing list, meeting time, and meeting place)

Discuss with the elder plans to contact these selected resources during the upcoming week(s). Determine the best day and time to make the initial contact; this day and time may be recorded on the piece of paper or index card containing the other information about the resource. Encourage the elder to write down important information received from the agency or individual resource person as a result of the contact. This information, also recorded on the piece of paper or index card, may be used for future reference and for discussion during the next session.

   Session wrap-up; enjoy a snack if desired.

ENDING THE SESSION:

   Share the basket.

   Talk about and confirm next session.

Explain to the elder that in the next session, his/her progress in contacting the identified resources will be discussed.

Ask the elder if there is an activity related to the unit topic that could be a part of the next session. If no new activities come to mind, ask which activities from the previous sessions could be repeated during the next session.

AFTER THE SESSION:

Write up comments.

It is a good idea for the leader to also keep a written record of the specific resources the elder intends to contact. This list will aid the leader in following up the referral process in the next session.

IDEAS FOR MODIFYING THE SESSION: If the elder cannot read or write or does not appear motivated to follow through on referrals, the leader may offer to help make the contact. This decision is left to the best judgment of the leader. If the leader helps make these contacts, he/she should follow the procedure as discussed below.

Assist in the process of contacting the agencies or individual resource person by dialing the phone and explaining that Mr. or Mrs. Jones is calling to inquire about the service. Then give the phone to the elder to make the actual inquiry.

It may be appropriate to ask the resource agency or person to make the initial contact with the elder. If so, the leader should be certain the elder has given permission for this contact to be made.

TIPS FOR SAFETY: No safety tips are needed. The leader is encouraged to display patience and understanding, as the elder may be very hesitant in responding to this session.

CHAPTER 6

Craft
Activity Plans

UNIT NAME: Crafts

ACTIVITY PLAN 2: MAKING BREAD DOUGH CRAFTS (The first activity in all recreation units should be "Assessing Recreation Interests." See pages 55 to 57.)

PURPOSE OF ACTIVITY: To teach a new craft idea and create an interest in this activity. Since the activity utilizes various cooking skills, it may also be useful for maintaining or increasing independence in preparing meals.

DESCRIPTION OF ACTIVITY: The leader will explain how to make bread dough crafts and involve the elder in making bread dough ornaments. The leader is encouraged to try other bread dough craft ideas as well.

BENEFITS OF ACTIVITY: Making bread dough crafts is fun! This activity also provides opportunities to exercise hand and arm muscles, express oneself creatively, experience a sense of accomplishment, and share a skill with another person. The crafts can be given as gifts or sold at craft shows, fairs, bazaars, etc.

BEFORE THE SESSION:

   Things to do

It is a good idea for the leader to make sample bread dough ornaments for demonstration. This gives the elder a chance to see the finished product and the leader a chance to practice the activity. Experimenting with other simple shapes, such as beads, buttons, napkin rings, and rope initials is encouraged. More advanced projects can include baskets, wreaths for candles, and small picture frames.

Things to take

Ingredients for bread dough:

   4 cups all-purpose flour (do not use self-rising flour)
   1 cup salt
   1½ cups water

(Note: The recipe should not be doubled as kneading becomes too difficult. It may be halved successfully, however.)

Additional materials:

   Baking sheet, covered with aluminum foil if desired
   Small bowl of water
   Rolling pin
   Wax paper
   Plastic bag or damp cloth
   Large mixing bowl
   Measuring cup
   1/2 cup extra flour
   Pancake turner
   Potholders
   Things to shape, mark, and mold the ornament such as cookie cutters,
      pizza cutter, fork, toothpicks, knife

WHAT TO DO DURING THE SESSION:

   Greeting and opening chat; pay attention to any immediate needs.

   Complete any unfinished business from previous session.

   Explain the session's activities.

Ask the elder to gather any cookie cutters that he/she would like to use for the project.

   Do activities.

The elder will perform the following steps with the help of the leader, as needed:

1. Combine flour and salt. Gradually add water, stirring to form a ball of dough.

2. On a lightly floured surface (wax paper may be used to protect surface), knead dough 10 minutes or until dough is smooth but firm. If dough is too sticky, knead in a small amount of flour; if too dry, work in a bit of water. Keep extra dough in a damp cloth or plastic bag as pieces of the mixture are pinched off to be shaped into ornaments.

3. Shape dough in desired forms. The easiest way to start designing is with a cookie cutter. Dough can also be shaped with hands, however. Roll out a small amount of dough about 1/4 inch thick. Start creating! If joining one piece of dough to another, prick surfaces to be joined lightly with a toothpick. Moisten both surfaces slightly with water and press together firmly.

4. To ensure even baking and to prevent the ornaments from swelling too much as they bake, punch holes or make deep cuts in all of the thick portions of each ornament. Try to make such holes and cuts part of the decoration's design. The easiest way to hang the ornament is to poke a hole with a pencil in the ornament before baking. A string or yarn can later be threaded through the hole for hanging.

5. Using a pancake turner, transfer the ornaments onto the baking sheet. Bake at 350 degrees until golden brown. This may take only 15 to 20 minutes, but the time will vary, depending on the thickness of the ornaments--so watch them carefully. If a piece bubbles during baking, pull out the baking sheet, poke a hole in the ornament with a toothpick, and return baking sheet to the oven. After baking, let ornaments cool thoroughly. Ornaments can also air-dry, instead of baking, for approximately 48 hours.

Session wrap-up; enjoy a snack if desired.

Select a dry place in which to store the ornaments until the next session ("Decorating Bread Dough Crafts").

ENDING THE SESSION:

Share the basket.

Talk about and confirm next session.

The leader may want to ask the elder if he/she has any supplies on hand that could be used in the next session, "Decorating Bread Dough Crafts." Also, the leader should ask the elder about sensitivity to the use of painting and/or sealing materials.

AFTER THE SESSION:

   Write up comments.

IDEAS FOR MODIFYING THE ACTIVITY: There are many possible creations. Use your imagination!

The visually impaired can be encouraged to feel the texture (roughness, hardness), size, shape, details, etc. The handles of kitchen utensils may be built up by wrapping or padding, thus making them easier to grasp. For sensitive skin, plastic gloves may be utilized. Powdering the inside of the glove helps to avoid moisture buildup.

The leader might want to have the dough mixed in advance. The elder could help knead and shape it. Not all individuals may be able to mix the dough, and this will reduce the number of items to take.

TIPS FOR SAFETY: Monitor use of utensils, oven, and materials. Make sure any spills are quickly cleaned off the floor. Provide adequate lighting and space.

UNIT NAME: Crafts

ACTIVITY PLAN 3: DECORATING BREAD DOUGH CRAFTS

PURPOSE OF ACTIVITY: To put finishing touches on bread dough ornaments made in the previous visit, "Making Bread Dough Crafts." To maintain and/or strengthen interest in this craft idea.

DESCRIPTION OF ACTIVITY: The bread dough ornaments made during a previous session will be finished. The leader will provide assistance, as necessary, with painting and sealing the ornaments.

BENEFITS OF ACTIVITY: This session provides an excellent opportunity for individual creative expression. It can also provide a sense of accomplishment and satisfaction as the final product is viewed. Painting and sealing the ornaments involves small-muscle manipulation skills--good exercise for hand and arm muscles.

BEFORE THE SESSION:

   Things to do

It is a good idea to finish some sample ornaments for demonstration. Perhaps ornaments prepared for the previous session, "Making Bread Dough Crafts," could be painted and sealed for this purpose. The leader may also be able to collect sample bread dough crafts created by others and show these finished products to the elder.

Things to take

Water-soluble paint--tempera, watercolor, acrylics
Powdered soap or detergent
Newspaper, or something to protect working space
Small brushes
Water bowls
Container for brushes, such as a tin can
Sealer--shellac, varnish, polyurethane, lacquer, etc.
Note: Spray-type sealer is recommended. The brush-on type may be slightly less expensive, but the spray is usually faster and easier to use. However, refer to precautions noted in the TIPS For SAFETY section of this plan.

WHAT TO DO DURING THE SESSION:

Greeting and opening chat; pay attention to any immediate needs.

Complete any unfinished business from previous session.

Ornaments made from previous visit should be gathered. If ornaments have softened somewhat, they may be placed in an oven at 200 degrees and baked for about 15 minutes to re-dry. Ornaments can cool while today's visit is explained and prepared.

Explain the session's activities.

Explain the purpose for sealing the ornaments--to protect against moisture and humidity. Painting or otherwise decorating the ornaments, however, is personal preference. Even the natural dough color looks attractive after sealing. Perhaps the elder will prefer to paint some and leave others natural.

Do activities.

Make sure the ornament is completely dry before decorating or sealing. If desired, the ornament can be painted. If painting, one color or several colors may be used on one ornament. Use your imagination and have fun!

To clean brushes, put powdered soap or detergent in a small container and add enough water to dissolve the soap, making a paste. Work the bristles of the brush in the paste. Rinse out the brush with water. Brushes can be stored in a tin can, oatmeal carton. etc., with the bristles up and not leaning against the side of the carton.

After painting, the ornament is finished off with a protective coating of varnish, shellac, polyurethane, or other sealer. The spray-type sealer is recommended because there will be no brushes to clean and the ornament dries quickly. Two coats are recommended. Make sure painting is thoroughly dry before sealer is applied.

Session wrap-up; enjoy a snack if desired.

During this time discuss plans for using the ornaments and the possibility of making additional bread dough crafts.

ENDING THE SESSION:

Share the basket.

Talk about and confirm next session.

AFTER THE SESSION:

Write up comments.

IDEAS FOR MODIFYING THE ACTIVITY: Various ideas for modifying the activity have been discussed throughout the activity plan. In addition, the leader may need to demonstrate techniques before the elder attempts the task. This may include actually physically guiding the elder's hands through the desired motion, particularly if he/she is visually impaired. Select simple decorating and/or painting ideas, perhaps limiting the use of colors.

For sensitive skin, use plastic gloves. Powder the inside of the glove to avoid moisture buildup. An apron or smock may also be used for protecting clothes from messy projects.

TIPS FOR SAFETY: Monitor use of all tools and utensils. Make sure any spills or other potential hazards are quickly cleaned up. Provide adequate lighting, space, and ventilation. Because of the possibility of respiratory problems, water-based paints are recommended, and aerosol products should be used with caution. The leader should spray on the finish sealer if the elder has respiratory problems. If both have respiratory problems, avoid the use of aerosol sprays.

UNIT NAME: Crafts

ACTIVITY PLAN 4: SOCK DOLLS*

PURPOSE OF ACTIVITY: To create something for personal enjoyment and for sharing with others. This project helps one understand the possibilities for using simple materials to create interesting projects. Making folk toys, such as sock dolls, may also encourage the elder to talk about toys of his/her childhood.

DESCRIPTION OF ACTIVITY: The leader will explain the procedure for making the sock doll, help the host select a sock to be used, and then assist the elder in making the sock doll, as needed.

BENEFITS OF ACTIVITY: Like most folk toys, there is no right or wrong way to construct the sock doll. This project encourages creativity and imagination. It also requires some coordination and use of small hand and arm muscles. Simple sewing skills are necessary to complete this project. Sewing may be a familiar skill to this person, thus helping to maintain and/or rekindle a previous interest. If not, this project will introduce a new experience. Folk toys can be given as birthday presents and Christmas presents or sold at bazaars, crafts shows, etc.

*From Stout, Jane A. Folk toys: Toys made by people for people! Ames, IA: Cooperative Extension Service, Iowa State University, 1982. Illustration and portions reprinted by permission.

BEFORE THE SESSION:

   Things to take

It is a good idea for the leader to make a sample sock doll prior
to the session. This gives the elder a chance to see the finished
product and the leader a chance to practice the activity. Try various
colors of socks and add various features to make each doll a little
different.

   Things to take

Scissors
Sewing needle
Thread or embroidery floss
Ribbon or some similar type of trim
Stuffing (polyester, cotton, or cut-up nylon hose)
Material scraps, such as felt, to be used as features
One or two socks (the elder may also be able to provide a sock)

WHAT TO DO DURING THE SESSION:

   Greeting and opening chat; pay attention to any immediate needs.

   Complete any unfinished business from previous session.

   Explain the session's activities.

After the activity is briefly explained, ask the elder to locate a
sock to use for the sock doll. The elder may also be able to help
provide some of the materials for stuffing, such as old nylon hose.

   Do activities.

As mentioned earlier, there is no right or wrong way to construct
a sock doll. The following instructions are just one way to create
the cuddly character.[*]

1. Fold the sock (as shown in the diagram) so that the heel lies
    flat at the top. Cut the ankle portion in half lengthwise.

2. Horizontally, cut off about half of the ankle to use for arms
    later. Sew up the remainder of the ankle to create legs.

3. Cut off the toe of the sock to create a stuffing hole.

4. Sew ribbon or a similar trim or string securely around the foot
    of the sock to form a neck. Stuff and attach "arms" (that part
    of the ankle cut off earlier). Stuff remainder of the doll.
    The heel of the sock will bulge out to form the doll's bottom.

5. Reattach the toe as a cap for the doll. Add features and, if
   desired, clothes.

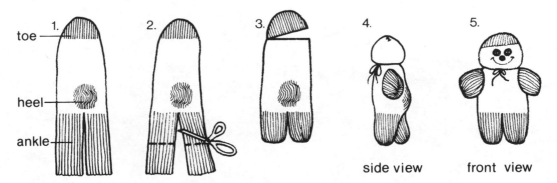

Session wrap-up; enjoy a snack if desired.

ENDING THE SESSION:

Share the basket.

Talk about and confirm next session.

AFTER THE SESSION:

Write up comments.

IDEAS FOR MODIFYING THE ACTIVITY: The sewing used in this project
may require the hands to be held stiffly for too long a period. Thus,
allow for necessary periods of rest. A thimble, preferably a leather
one, may be helpful.

An embroidery needle and embroidery thread may be used instead of
a regular-size needle and thread; they will be larger and easier to
use.

Lines may be traced onto the sock so that the individual will have
a pattern to follow as he/she cuts.

TIPS FOR SAFETY: Make sure the work space is well lighted. Monitor
the use of tools such as scissors and needles. Stress that there
is no hurry to finish the project, since hurrying sometimes leads
to accidents.

If the doll will be given as a gift to a small child, do not use buttons
or other items that could be pulled off and swallowed.

UNIT NAME: Crafts

ACTIVITY PLAN 5: DECORATED JARS

PURPOSE OF ACTIVITY: To introduce a simple craft idea that utilizes recycled materials and yet is a pleasurable and satisfying project to complete and enjoy.

DESCRIPTION OF ACTIVITY: The leader will explain various ways to decorate jars and will involve the elder in the process of making one or two jars.

BENEFITS OF ACTIVITY: This craft idea is simple, inexpensive, and easy to make but very satisfying. It provides opportunities for demonstrating creativity, imagination, and personal expression. This craft project is ideal for undertaking with another older person, students, neighbors, or grandchildren. Decorated jars can be kept for personal use, given as birthday presents or Christmas presents, sold at bazaars, etc.

BEFORE THE SESSION:

   Things to do

It is a good idea for the leader to decorate a jar prior to the session. This gives the elder a chance to see the finished product and the leader a chance to practice the activity. The leader is encouraged to try various ways of decorating the jars.

Things to take

Acrylic paints (if desired and if obtainable)
Paint brush(es) (if painting is desired)
Permanent marking pens (if painting is desired)
Material scraps
Pinking shears
Measuring tape
Various lengths of colored ribbon or yarn
White glue
Other materials that could be used for decorating, as desired
Old pickle jars, peanut butter jars, baby food jars, other wide-mouth
  jars--lids included

WHAT TO DO DURING THE SESSION:

   Greeting and opening chat; pay attention to any immediate needs.

   Complete any unfinished business from previous session.

   Explain the session's activities.

After briefly explaining the activity, ask the elder to locate jars
he/she would like to use for this project.

   Do activities.

Jars and lids should be clean. Jars may be painted with various sayings
and designs, if desired. Patterns may be drawn on jars initially
with permanent marking pens. Design ideas may be gathered by looking
at magazines, coloring books, cookie cutters, etc. Simple designs
(such as stripes) and shapes are recommended.

While paint dries, cut circles from material scraps, using pinking shears. Circles should measure at least 1½ to 2 inches wider than the lid for each jar. Center material circle on the jar lid and glue in place (both the top and the sides of the lid should have glue applied to them). Be sure to use glue sparingly. Allow lid and jar to dry thoroughly.

Cut ribbon or yarn long enough to encircle the jar lid and still have enough length for tying a bow. The width of ribbon depends on the width of the lid band. Most often used is 1/4- to 1/2-inch ribbon.

Material circles need not be glued but simply tied onto the lid, if desired. Also, the jar lid can be slightly padded with cotton or polyester stuffing before attaching the material if desired.

Session wrap-up; enjoy a snack if desired.

ENDING THE SESSION:

Share the basket.

Talk about and confirm next session.

AFTER THE SESSION:

Write up comments.

IDEAS FOR MODIFYING THE ACTIVITY: Fabric may be inserted into the center of a thick book and cut with bent-handle scissors. Some people may find squeeze scissors or electric scissors easier to work with.

TIPS FOR SAFETY: Make sure the work space is of adequate size and well lit. Monitor the handling of all materials, especially the scissors and jars, and demonstrate proper use if necessary. Allow for periods of rest as needed and enjoy!

UNIT NAME: Crafts

ACTIVITY PLAN 6: QUIET BOOK*

PURPOSE OF ACTIVITY: To provide a fun and mentally challenging activity.

DESCRIPTION OF ACTIVITY: Explain the procedure for making a quiet book, introduce the materials to be used, and involve the elder in the construction of this craft project.

BENEFITS OF ACTIVITY: Making the quiet book provides opportunities for creative expression and use of imagination. This craft project is easy to construct, but it is mentally challenging and results in a very individualized product. Making the book stimulates sensory involvement of the elder and requires hand-eye coordination. This craft project can be made as a gift for a young child (such as a grandchild), can be sold at bazaars or craft fairs, or can be donated to various community services in which young children participate, such as day-care centers, church nurseries, hospital waiting areas. Thus, the participant enjoys a feeling of importance and of service to others.

BEFORE THE SESSION:

   Things to do

*From Stout, Jane A. <u>Crafts for the leisure years</u>. Ames, IA: Cooperative Extension Service, Iowa State University, 1980. Illustration and portions reprinted by permission.

It is a good idea for the leader to make a quiet book prior to the visit. This gives the elder a chance to view the finished product and the leader a chance to practice.

Things to take

Plain or light-colored material scraps
A variety of materials of different textures
Needle
Thread
Scissors (preferably pinking shears)
Glue
Sewing machine (optional)
Used clothes (optional)
Assorted buttons, sewing notions, zippers, figured material

WHAT TO DO DURING THE SESSION:

Greeting and opening chat; pay attention to any immediate needs.

Complete any unfinished business from previous session.

Explain the session's activities.

After the project is briefly explained, ask the elder to locate any of the supplies needed for this craft project that he/she would like to use.

Do activities.

Cut six pieces of material into rectangles of equal size; pinking shears will produce a nice edge. Sew down the center of the pile, by hand or with machine, making a hinged booklet of 12 pages.

On each page, attach an item in an appropriate manner (by sewing or gluing) that has texture or interest to a child. The pages of the book may vary greatly from simply colors and textures to actual learning items such as zippers and buttons. Refer to the illustrations at the end of this activity plan for suggestions and ideas.

Hint: If access to used clothes is possible, simply cut off and glue down a pocket, zipper, button track, etc.

Session wrap-up; enjoy a snack if desired.

The leader should encourage the elder to identify various individuals or organizations who might enjoy receiving a quiet book as a gift and/or discuss other plans for using this craft idea.

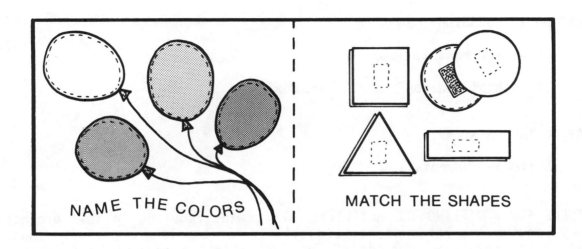

NAME THE COLORS   MATCH THE SHAPES

WHAT TIME IS IT?   OPEN

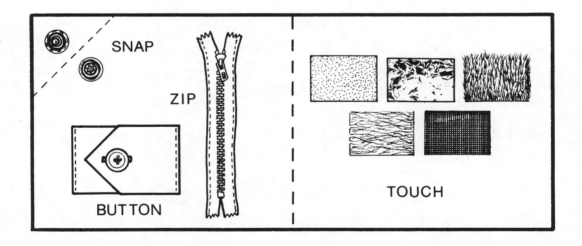

SNAP   ZIP   TOUCH

BUTTON

ENDING THE SESSION:

Share the basket.

Talk about and confirm next session.

AFTER THE SESSION:

Write up comments.

IDEAS FOR MODIFYING THE ACTIVITY: The sewing required in this project may require the hands to be held stiffly for too long a period. Thus, allow for necessary periods of rest. A thimble, preferably a leather one, may be helpful. It might also be helpful to use gluing instead of sewing whenever possible. Fewer pages or additional pages may be added to the quiet book as desired.

TIPS FOR SAFETY: Make sure the work space is well lighted. This area should be clear before ending the session. Monitor the use of tools such as scissors, needle, sewing machine. Allow for plenty of time to complete the project so that there is no need to hurry. This project could be finished during the beginning of the next session.

UNIT NAME: Crafts

ACTIVITY PLAN 7: BLOCK PRINTING

PURPOSE OF ACTIVITY: To introduce simple printing techniques and to demonstrate that art materials need not be limited.

DESCRIPTION OF ACTIVITY: The leader will introduce the craft of printing and involve the elder in printmaking with a variety of familiar materials.

BENEFITS OF ACTIVITY: Block printing is ideal for the beginner because it is simple and inexpensive, yet its possibilities can be numerous and complex enough to challenge the experienced craft person. Block printing will stimulate sensory involvement--seeing, touching, smelling--and provide opportunities to use imagination and creativity. Block printing may be used on wall hangings, tote bags, book covers, wrapping paper, greeting cards, and in many other ways.

BEFORE THE SESSION:

   Things to do

It is a good idea for the leader to make a few block printing projects prior to the session. This gives the elder a chance to see the finished product and the leader a chance to practice the activity. The leader is encouraged to try various objects for printing. The objects that were most successful or satisfying may be recommended for use.

Things to take

Several common objects such as scrap wood, jar lids, corks, spools,
    kitchen utensils
Select two or more of these: raw onion, green pepper, potato, carrot,
    etc.
Paring knife
Tissue paper (a sheet or two)
Plain wrapping paper (a sheet or two)
Construction paper (white and/or colored)
Any type of drawing paper that does not have a slick surface
Newspaper
Tempera paints and/or a water-based block printing ink
Scissors
Several lids from old jars

WHAT TO DO DURING THE SESSION:

Greeting and opening chat; pay attention to any immediate needs.

Complete any unfinished business from previous session.

Explain the session's activities.

The leader should explain that block printing is one of the oldest
crafts. The process used today is similar to the one used nearly
4,000 years ago. After the activity is briefly explained, ask the
elder to think of any objects that might be used for printing. Gather
whatever objects are available and use them.

Do activities.

Cover the table or work area with several layers of newspaper. If
using raw vegetables, such as an onion, green pepper, carrot, or potato,
cut a cross section of each. Also, a notch or simple shape may be
cut from the potatoes and carrots before printing with them. Try
experimenting with both--printing with a cross section of the vegetable
as well as a notched one.

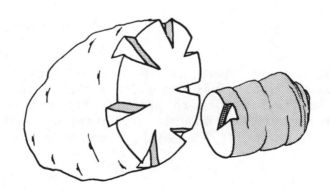

Using tempera paints (as many colors as desired) or a water-based block printing ink, put a tiny "puddle" of paint on a piece of paper or an old jar lid. (Use a separate piece of paper or jar lid for each color.) Using an object of choice, gently push the side that will be used for printing into the paint, dab it on the edge of the paint paper once or twice to get rid of some of the extra paint, and then print it by laying it on a piece of paper and pressing it slightly. If the print is too light after the object is removed, either the object needs more paint or ink or more pressure needs to be applied. If the print is messy or the block slides, too much paint/ink may have been used. Re-ink the object after each print. Try block printing on tissue and wrapping paper, brown paper-sack paper, white and/or colored construction paper, or any type of drawing paper that does not have a slick surface.

Hints and suggestions:

Do not cut the raw vegetables too much ahead of time, as the cut edges will shrink quickly. When they shrink the edges will be uneven and will not print well.

Select colors for paper that will contrast well with the colors of paint or ink you have available.

Lines and shapes should be cut only slightly into the raw potato or carrot. Shallow cuts will print just fine. If too much paint gets on the carrot or potato and fills in the shallow cuts, just wipe it off with a piece of facial tissue.

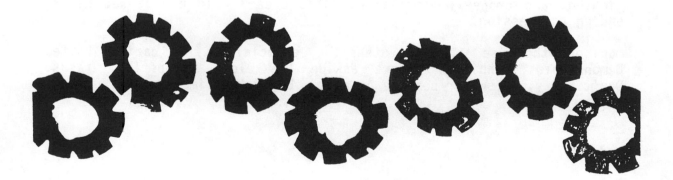

Session wrap-up; enjoy a snack if desired.

ENDING THE SESSION:

Share the basket.

Talk about and confirm next session.

AFTER THE SESSION:

Write up comments.

IDEAS FOR MODIFYING THE ACTIVITY: Paint or ink may also be applied to the object for printing using a paint brush, stamp pad, or brayer (rubber roller).

The leader may prefer to cut the raw vegetables to avoid the use of the knife by the elder.

Use simple shapes and strongly contrasting colors. Big shapes will fill the space more easily and will be less tedious to work with.

Chair arms may be built up with folded towels or other padding so that elbows are supported.

TIPS FOR SAFETY: Make sure the work area is of adequate size, well lighted, and properly ventilated. This area should be cleaned before ending the session.

Monitor the use of all utensils, especially the paring knife. Demonstrate techniques before asking the elder to perform tasks. Don't hurry; allow for periods of rest. Enjoy the time together!

REFERENCES AND RESOURCES

Bodkin, C., Leibowitz, H., & Weiner, D. Crafts for your leisure years. Boston: Houghton Mifflin, 1976.

Colin, P., & Lippman, D. Craft sources. New York: M. Evans, 1975.

Cook, C. Unique art lessons and special projects for the elementary classroom. West Nyack, NY: Parker, 1975.

Craig, J. E. Creative art activities. Scranton, PA: International Textbook, 1967.

Eben, L. E. 129 art lessons in 26 media. West Nyack, NY: Parker, 1977.

Eckstein, A. A. How to make treasures from trash: Recycling can be beautiful. Nashville, TN: Ingram, 1972.

Gault, E., & Sykes, S. Crafts for the disabled. New York: Thomas Y. Crowell, 1979.

Gooch, P. H. Ideas for art teachers. New York: Van Nostrand Reinhold, 1972.

Gould, E., & Gould, L. Crafts for the elderly. Springfield, IL: Charles C. Thomas, 1976.

Lyon, M. Crafts for the aging: A working manual for directors of handicraft programs for older people. New York: American Craftsman's Council, 1962.

Office of Extension Information. Eyes of God--"Ojos de Dios." Manhattan, KS: Kansas State University, TVC9-72.

Peck, R. L. Best of teacher's arts and crafts workshop. West Nyack, NY: Parker, 1974.

Rich, M. K. Handicrafts for homebound handicapped. Springfield, IL: Charles C. Thomas, 1960.

Rissell, W. A. Craftwork the handicapped elderly can make and sell. Springfield, IL: Charles C. Thomas, 1981.

Sanderson, G. S. Elementary teacher's art ideas desk book. West Nyack, NY: Parker, 1974.

Shivers, J. S., & Fait, H. F. Plastic and graphic arts. In Recreational service for the aging (pp. 167-190). Philadelphia: Lea & Febiger, 1980.

Stout, J. A. Crafts for the leisure years. Ames, IA: Cooperative Extension Service, Iowa State University, 1980.

_____. Folk toys: Toys made by people for people! Ames, IA: Cooperative Extension Service, Iowa State University, 1982.

Tague, J. (Ed.). Programming trends in therapeutic recreation. Denton, TX: Creative Leisure Services.

Tritten, G. Art techniques for children. New York: Reinhold, 1966.

Adapted activity equipment

One-Handed Embroidery Frame
A holder for knitting, crocheting, and embroidery; most useful for embroidery.
Supplier: Cleo Living Aids

Rake Knitting Frame
For the one-handed person doing simple knitting. The frames come in a variety of sizes. (The 13" size is suitable for knitting an adult stocking cap.)
Supplier: Cleo Living Aids

Needle Threader
For use by a one-handed person who has difficulty threading a needle but has good vision; for sewing thread only.
Supplier: Fred Sammons Inc.

Left-handed Scissors
For someone who cannot use the right hand for cutting.
Supplier: Fred Sammons Inc.
Note: Children's blunt scissors can also be used but only for paper. Electric scissors are useful for a well-coordinated person. Left-handed scissors are also available, in various sizes, in most fabric stores and notion stores.

Scissors for Handicapped
For cutting by those who have diminished hand strength or those whose hand dominance has changed. It has a built-up plastic handle; also useful for gardening.
Supplier: Fred Sammons Inc.

Fiberglass Measuring Tape
Tactile indications are reinforced holes.
Supplier: American Foundation for the Blind

Leather Holding Mitt
To assist people with limited strength to hold tools such as sanding blocks, rolling pins, mallets, etc. The mitts come in various sizes.
Supplier: Fred Sammons Inc.

Comfort Utensil Holder
Good for the person having no useful grasp in either hand. It can
serve as a holder for small-handled tools such as paintbrushes, pencils,
stamping tools. It is available in various sizes. (This kind of
device is easy to make.)
Supplier: Fred Sammons Inc.

Adjustable Work Table
For supporting equipment for work; can be moved, raised, or set at
an angle; has a cut-out space for the user.
Supplier: G. E. Miller, Inc.

Pony Spring Clamps
For holding work pieces; easily used by a one-handed person who needs
to secure items to the table.
Supplier: Fred Sammons Inc.

Ja-Son Snip Loop Scissors
Made with a single plastic spring-loaded loop; for those who cannot
handle normal scissors because of strength or joint limitations;
designed for light cutting.
Supplier: Scott and Fetzer

Swivel Bench Vise
For attaching to a table for stabilization of equipment and work pieces.
(This is available in many hardware stores.)
Supplier: Sax Arts and Crafts

Sit-on Stitchery Frame
An adjustable sit-on frame for needlepoint; useful for the one-handed
or those with generalized weakness.
Supplier: Lee Wards

Talon Self-Threading Yarn Threader
For aid in threading fine or heavy yarn; helpful for those with visual
limitations or mild coordination problems.
Supplier: Donahue Sales (and fabric or yarn stores carrying Talon
products)

Suppliers[*]

Cleo Living Aids
3957 Mayfield Rd.
Cleveland, OH 44121

Donahue Sales
Talon Division of Textron
41 East 51st St.
New York, NY 10022

Fred Sammons Inc.
Box 32
Brookfield, IL 60315

Lee Wards
1200 St. Charles Rd.
Elgin, IL 60120

G. E. Miller, Inc.
484 South Broadway
Yonkers, NY 10705

Scott and Fetzer Company
Ja-Son Division, Dept. DCI
217 Long Hill Cross Roads
Shelton, CT 06484

Homemade and common items*

Can Holder
This tool stabilizes cans while the participant works. It is especially
useful for an uncoordinated or confused person. A cut-out circle
in the wood base holds the can, and the holder can be clamped to the
table.

Stabilizers
C-clamps, wood vises, clipboards, and bean bags are necessary for
uncoordinated or one-handed participants.

Spool Holder
This device stabilizes thread, lace, or string for an uncoordinated
or one-handed participant. The base is cut larger than the size of
the objects it is to hold and a dowel in the center holds the spool.
The base can be anchored to the table with a C-clamp.

Lapboard
This aid is available commercially and can be easily made. It is
useful for those who need arm support when sitting in a chair or for
those who have body-trunk instability. The board is also useful where
table aprons limit access to the work surface. It can be cut out
of 1/4" plywood or Masonite, and Velcro tape or leather straps can
be attached to the sides for fastening around wheelchair arms to
increase stability.

Clipboard
This is handy for holding writing paper and can also be used to
stabilize a small needlecraft project taped to a mat frame.

Stabilized Nail
The nail is hammered through the center of a wooden base, point up.
It is useful for shaping clay beads, holding a spool of thread to
keep it from rolling, or anchoring other items, such as the pomander
ball.

*These and other suggestions for adapted activtiy equipment are found
in Hamill, C. M., & Oliver, R. C. Therapeutic activities for the
handicapped elderly (Appendix B, pp. 261-265; Appendix E, pp. 275-278).
Rockville, MD: Aspen Systems Corporation, 1980. Reprinted with
permission of Aspen Publishers, Inc.

CHAPTER 7

Games Activity Plans

UNIT NAME: Games

ACTIVITY PLAN 2: SIMPLE CARD GAMES (The first activity in all recreation units should be "Assessing Recreation Interests." See pages 55 to 57.)

PURPOSE OF ACTIVITY: To introduce an activity that involves simple rules and yet is mentally challenging and requires some physical action.

DESCRIPTION OF ACTIVITY: The leader will explain how to play one or both simple card games (depending on time and interest) and involve the elder in playing the game(s).

BENEFITS OF ACTIVITY: Card games are a popular activity. These games involve simple rules but require observation and logical thinking, thus stimulating mental activity. The games also require some physical action, mostly hand and arm movement/coordination. Interaction with another person is also involved.

BEFORE THE SESSION:

Things to do

No preparations are necessary before this session. It is a good idea, however, for the leader to review the rules for the card games, perhaps playing them with another person just for practice (and fun!).

Things to take

One regular deck of 52 playing cards
Paper and pencil for recording game scores, if desired

WHAT TO DO DURING THE SESSION:

Greeting and opening chat; pay attention to any immediate needs.

Complete any unfinished business from previous session.

Explain the session's activities.

Interesting information about card games, such as that below, can
be shared while explaining the session's activities.

Many of today's popular card games began in different forms
thousands of years ago.

The original purpose of card games was to teach military strategy
to young warriors.

Card games are believed to have been first invented in either
ancient Egypt or India.

Card games first became popular among the ruling nobilities of
the Orient, and present-day cards still show the signs of their
noble origins in the face cards: king, queen, and jack.

Do activities.

The two card games to be presented are Go Boom and War.*

1. <u>Go Boom</u> (This game can be played with two or more people.):

The Deal: Seven cards are dealt to each player. The remaining cards
are placed in a pack face down on the table.

The Play: The first player begins by putting one card on the table,
face up. The second player must play a card that matches it, either
in value or in suit. For example, if the card is a six of diamonds,
either a diamond or a six must follow. If this is not possible, the
player must draw from the pack until finding a diamond or a six.
Then the second player puts down a card, and the game continues in
this manner.

The Scoring: The winner is the first player to get rid of all held
cards. If no player has won by the time the last card in the pack
has been drawn, the discards may be reshuffled and the drawing continued
until someone wins. The game may also end when the last card from
the pack is drawn, with the player holding the fewest cards declared
the winner.

*Adapted from <u>Book of 1000 family games</u>. Copyright 1971. The Reader's
Digest Association Inc. Used by permission.

2. War:

The Deal: Two players sit facing each other at a small table. One player shuffles the deck and deals out 26 cards to his opponent and keeps 26, thus dividing the deck into halves.

The Play: Both players turn their top cards over at the same time. The player with the high card takes both cards and puts them in a personal stack. (In this game, the ace is low and the king is high.) If the two cards turned up are the same (two sixes or two queens, for example), war is declared. Each player then turns up one more card, and the player with the high card of that pair takes all four cards. If again the cards are the same, it's "double war," and two additional cards are turned up, with the player who has the high card of the pair taking all three pairs and putting them at the bottom of his/her stack. The game goes on in this manner until one player has captured all of the cards--which may take quite awhile.

   Session wrap-up; enjoy a snack if desired.

ENDING THE SESSION:

   Share the basket.

   Talk about and confirm next session.

At the end of the session the leader and elder may decide to play one of these card games during the next session. This might be a fun way to start or end the session.

AFTER THE SESSION:

   Write up comments.

IDEAS FOR MODIFYING THE ACTIVITY: Card decks with large print and oversize decks are available from department stores and mail order companies. Braille playing cards are also available. For those who need assistance managing the cards, Hale (1981) suggests trying various grooved holders, available from self-help equipment firms, or a tray that hangs out of sight just below the table top. Battery-operated card shufflers and automatic card dealers are also available and might be helpful.

Possible resources to contact concerning these items include local hobby shops, discount stores, sporting goods stores, state commissions for the blind, and the National Foundation for the Blind. The occupational therapy department of a hospital is another good source. In addition, the local senior citizens center or parks and recreation department may be of assistance in locating these aids. (Check the resource list at the end of this unit for further assistance.)

One effective card holder suggested by Hale (1981) can be made by sawing slots 1 inch (2.5 cm) deep, in a piece of solid wood that is at least 2 inches (5 cm) thick. "A piece of felt or pimple rubber glued to the base will keep it from slipping" (Hale, 1981, p. 342).

The leader is encouraged to make any rule modifications appropriate and/or necessary. It may be necessary for the leader to do all of the shuffling and dealing of the cards.

Other card games may be substituted for the ones described in this session if desired.

TIPS FOR SAFETY: None needed, except a general attention to the well-being of the elder. The game(s) require concentration and memory and could create frustration. Make sure the elder is comfortably situated in the playing area and that it is well lighted.

UNIT NAME: Games

ACTIVITY PLAN 3: GUESSING GAMES

PURPOSE OF ACTIVITY: To introduce an activity that is both challenging and enjoyable.

DESCRIPTION OF ACTIVITY: The leader will explain how to play a guessing word game and engage the elder in playing this game. The participants may choose to try other similar guessing games.

BENEFITS OF ACTIVITY: Guessing games are fun and can be very challenging. Very little equipment or preparation is required, and these games provide an opportunity for informal interaction. This is also a good activity to enjoy with other friends, grandchildren, etc.

BEFORE THE SESSION:

Things to do

The leader prepares a list of sayings with the words scrambled for the Hidden Sayings* game. The leader prepares a number of names with the letters scrambled for the Scrambled People* game.

* From Hohenstein, Mary. Games for people of all ages. Minneapolis, MN: Bethany House Publishers. Copyright © 1980. Reprinted by permission.

Things to take

Paper
Pencils for both participants
Something to write on, such as a book or lapboard
Lists of scrambled sayings and names

WHAT TO DO DURING THE SESSION:

Greeting and opening chat; pay attention to any immediate needs.

Complete any unfinished business from previous session.

Explain the session's activities.

Do activities.

1. Hidden Sayings:

The objective of this game is to find the hidden sayings. The leader gives the elder a copy of a list of famous or popular sayings, proverbs, adages, golden rules, etc., which has been written in such a way that it is difficult to identify. For example, the saying "The early bird catches the worm" could be written as "THEE ARL YBI RDCA TCHE STH EWO RM."

The elder is encouraged to decipher as many sayings as possible. If desired, the elder can also prepare a list of hidden sayings for the leader to decipher. The leader and elder would then exchange lists and try to decipher the sayings.

Use very familiar/well-known sayings until the elder becomes comfortable with how the game is played. More challenging sayings may then be utilized.

2. Scrambled People:

The object of this game is to unscramble the names. The leader chooses a category, such as authors, actors, biblical people, historical figures, current events figures, friends. A number of names are prepared and their letters are scrambled. For example, under the category of historical figures, Ronald Reagan's name might be presented as DONRLA AGRAEN. (Somewhere, perhaps on the back of the list, the answers should be written.)

The leader describes the category and presents the first scrambled name. The elder is encouraged to unscramble as many names as possible. If desired, the elder can also prepare a list of scrambled names under one of the categories for the leader to unscramble. The leader and elder would then exchange lists and see who could unscramble the most names. The elder might also be given a choice as to which category will be used.

Again, use very familiar/well-known people until the elder becomes comfortable with how the game is played. More challenging names may then be utilized.

Session wrap-up; enjoy a snack if desired.

ENDING THE SESSION:

Share the basket.

Talk about and confirm next session.

If desired, the leader and elder might plan to prepare a list of hidden sayings and/or scrambled people to exchange and decipher during the next session. This idea would involve the elder in a small activity during the week and would be a fun way to begin the next session.

AFTER THE SESSION:

Write up comments.

IDEAS FOR MODIFYING THE ACTIVITY:

1. Instead of sayings, titles of books or songs can be used. As stated, these should be familiar ones.

2. First lines of poems or songs can also be used, or scripture passages. A limit should be set on the number of words if such first lines or verses are used.

Sayings and/or names should be written in large letters if the participant is visually impaired. Simple sayings and names should be used if reading and writing skills are weak. (If the elder has limited reading/writing ability, these games will probably not be suitable and the leader may elect to choose another activity plan from this unit.)

TIPS FOR SAFETY: None needed, except for a general attention to the participant's well-being. Watch for signs that the elder is tiring of the activity or is frustrated and/or confused. Make sure the elder is comfortable in the playing area and that it is well lighted.

UNIT NAME: Games

ACTIVITY PLAN 4: DOMINOES*

PURPOSE OF ACTIVITY: To involve the participant in a game of Dominoes and introduce variations to the basic game. Playing Dominoes may be a new experience, or this session may revive interest in a familiar activity.

DESCRIPTION OF ACTIVITY: The leader will review, or explain for the first time, the procedures for playing Dominoes. After the basic game is played, variations may be introduced if desired.

BENEFITS OF ACTIVITY: The game of Dominoes involves interaction with another person and stresses easygoing fun. The game also requires alertness and observation, thus providing mental stimulation. Playing Dominoes exercises the hand and arm muscles and involves coordination of these muscles. The game can be challenging and played as competitively as desired.

BEFORE THE SESSION:

   Things to do

The leader should practice the game(s) with another individual if possible. If not, practice repeating the directions for the games

*All variations of Dominoes presented in this session plan are adapted from <u>Book of 1000 Family Games</u>. Copyright ©1971. The Reader's Digest Association Inc. Used by permission.

and setting up the Dominoes. It is important that the leader know how to play Dominoes.

Things to take

A standard set of Double-Six Dominoes
Paper and pencils for keeping score

WHAT TO DO DURING THE SESSION:

Greeting and opening chat; pay attention to any immediate needs.

Complete any unfinished business from previous session.

Explain the session's activities.

Do activities.

Objective: There are many variations of Dominoes, but most games share a common objective--to try to rid the hand of all dominoes before an opponent can do so.

Ranking of Suits: In Dominoes, "suit" and number mean the same thing. There are seven doubles: the double blank, zero-zero; the double one, one-one; two-two; three-three; four-four; five-five; and six-six. In addition, there are 21 dominoes with each end showing a different number: for instance, six-five; four-one; three-blank. A domino with two different numbers belongs to two suits: A six-five, for example, belongs to both the six suit and the five suit. A double--since both ends are the same--belongs to only one suit.

Preparation: The set of dominoes is placed face down on the table and thoroughly mixed, a process like that of shuffling in a game of cards. Each player draws to determine who has the first play; high wins, the double six being highest. An appropriate number of dominoes, or "bones," are then drawn by each player to form playing hands; this number varies, depending on the specific game and the number of players in the game. The remaining dominoes are kept face down in what is known as the "boneyard," which is situated nearby but away from the center of the table. One's hand is concealed from opponents, generally by standing the dominoes on end directly in front of you so that only you can see their values.

1. Block Dominoes:

There are two players; for example, Robert and Lewis. Each draws seven dominoes to form playing hands. The boneyard cannot be used again and is moved off to the side of the table. The winner of the draw for first play, Robert, takes any domino from his hand and places it face up in the center of the table. Lewis must follow suit; in other words, he must match one of the ends of the domino on the board

with a number from his hand. For example, if the first domino is
a two-two, any domino with a two at one end will do. Should Lewis
hold, say, the two-one, he places it with the two end touching either
end of the two-two. See illustration to follow this sequence of plays.
Robert then takes his second turn. Before him there are two dominoes;
at one end of the row there is a two (the unplayed end of the two-two)
and at the other end there is a one. Any domino with a two or a one
at either end can now be played.

In the above fashion, the players alternate turns in building a row
of dominoes across the table, the dominoes always linked by numbers
of the same suit. If one player cannot follow suit, he calls out,
"Go!" thus signaling his opponent to make another play. If the blocked
player still cannot follow suit after this second play, he must again
call "Go!" and continue to do so for as long as he is blocked.

When either Robert or Lewis plays off all of his dominoes, the game
ends. His opponent counts up the points on all of the dominoes he
still holds; the sum goes to the winner as his score for that hand.
In the case where both Robert and Lewis are blocked, they each count
up the points remaining in their hands. The one with the fewest points
is winner and collects the difference in points between the two hands.
After each hand both draw new hands of seven from the boneyard, and
the loser of the previous hand begins play in the next game. The
grand game-winning total is generally 50 points.

2. Draw Dominoes:

In Draw Dominoes, the player who is blocked must continue to draw
from the boneyard until he/she gets a playable domino. Two dominoes
must stay in the boneyard; in other words, the drawing stops when
only two dominoes remain in the boneyard.

3. All Fives:

All Fives is best with two or three players, but may be played with
as many as five. All aspects of the game with respect to the draw,
the boneyard, the requirements to follow suit, and the draw from the

boneyard when unable to follow suit are the same as described for
Draw Dominoes. However, even when a player can follow suit, the option
exists to pass the turn and draw one domino from the boneyard in order
to improve one's hand.

First play is made by the person holding the highest doublet--the
six-six being highest--which is placed face up in the center of the
table. Should no one have a doublet, the players take turns drawing
from the boneyard until someone receives one. In a two-player game,
each person draws seven dominoes to begin; when more than two play,
each draws five.

All Fives differs from ordinary Dominoes in that points can be scored
during the play. The initial doublet is built on both at the ends
and the sides, resulting in a cross formation with four ends, rather
than the two of a simple straight row. However, all doublets after
the first may be built on only at their sides, and both ends count
in the total. Should a player position a domino that makes the outside
number in all open arms of the chain total a sum divisible by five,
such as 15, 20, 25, he/she receives that number of points automatically.
Of course, the rule governing the matching of suits in ordinary dominoes
also applies in All Fives; that is, a two can only be played on a
two, a blank only adjoining a blank, a six only next to a six, and
so forth.

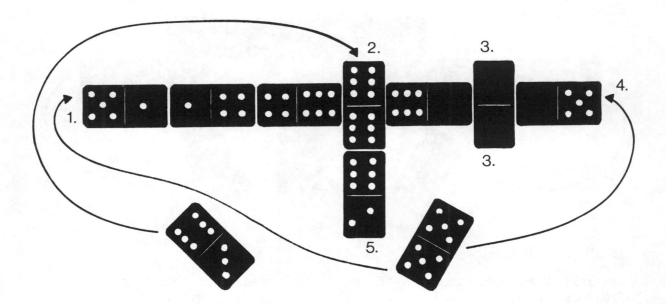

As in Block Dominoes, the first player to play all of the dominoes
in his/her hand collects all of the points still held by the opponent,
rounded off to the nearest five. For instance, if an opponent holds
13, 14, 16, or 17 points, the score is written as 15. If the play
is blocked, the low player subtracts his/her points from those of
the high player, again rounding off the score to the nearest five.
Points scored during play are added up with those received for ridding

oneself of all dominoes. After each game, the dominoes are collected, turned face down, mixed, and a new hand is drawn. Generally the first player to reach 100 points wins the game.

Practice counting points shown in the illustration before playing the double five or six-three dominoes.

       (#1) 5 pts from the 5-1 end
       (#2) 6 pts from the original 6-6 domino
       (#3) 0 pts from the two ends of the double-blank
       (#4) 5 pts from the 5-blank end
       (#5) <u>2 pts</u> from the 6-2 end
            18 points total before play

Playing the double five on either end of the chain would result in 18 - 5 + 10 = 23 points, which is not a multiple of 5 and will not earn points. Playing the six-three on the six end of the original double six would result in 18 - 6 + 3 = 15, which is a multiple of 5, and this play would earn 15 points.

Session wrap-up; enjoy a snack if desired.

Discuss the variation of Dominoes enjoyed most.

ENDING THE SESSION:

Share the basket.

Talk about and confirm next session.

The leader and elder might plan to play a short game of one of the Dominoes variations at the beginning of the next session.

AFTER THE SESSION:

Write up comments.

IDEAS FOR MODIFYING THE ACTIVITY: There are several variations of the basic game of Block Dominoes; the leader is encouraged to introduce variations during the session as desired.

Oversize dominoes and dominoes with raised numbers are commercially available and may be helpful for those with visual problems. Check with local hobby shops or discount stores or contact a local senior citizens center regarding where these dominoes can be borrowed or purchased. Someone who works with wood may be able to make an oversize set of dominoes.

TIPS FOR SAFETY: No special tips are needed, just a general attention to the participant's well-being. Watch for signs of tiring. Make sure the elder is comfortable in the playing area and that it is well lighted.

UNIT NAME: Games

ACTIVITY PLAN 5: SOLITAIRE

PURPOSE OF ACTIVITY: To introduce a card game that can be played individually as well as with others.

DESCRIPTION OF ACTIVITY: The leader will explain how to play Solitaire* and observe the elder playing this game.   If time permits and if desired, both will play Double Solitaire.*

BENEFITS OF ACTIVITY: Card games are a popular activity requiring observation, concentration, and logical thinking.   Some physical action is required, mostly hand and arm movement and coordination.   In Double Solitaire, interaction with another person is also provided.

BEFORE THE SESSION:

   Things to do

The leader should review the rules for this card game prior to the session.   Play Double Solitaire with another person just for practice and fun.

   Things to take

Two regular decks of 52 playing cards.

*Adapted from Book of 1000 Family Games.   Copyright © 1971.   The Reader's Digest Association Inc. Used by permission.

WHAT TO DO DURING THE SESSION:

Greeting and opening chat; pay attention to any immediate needs.

Complete any unfinished business from previous session.

Explain the session's activities.

Do activities.

1. Solitaire:

Object: Each player tries to build completely the four suits in ascending order on the four foundation aces.

Ranking of Cards: Ace is low; king is high.

Preparation and Deal: Of the many variations of Solitaire the most widely played form is described here. After shuffling, the player deals a line of seven cards from left to right--the first card face up, the rest face down. Now repeat the process, but skip the first card and place a card face up on the second card from the left and cards face down on the remaining piles.

Again the deal is repeated--first card up, the remainder down--this time beginning with pile number three. The deal continues until only one card remains, which is laid face up on the seventh pile. The resulting arrangement--the "Tableau"--is seven piles, each capped by a face-up card. The piles contain one, two, three, four, five, six, and seven cards, respectively--28 cards in all. The 24 remaining cards are put aside as a stock for later use.

Play: Because only the face-up cards can be manipulated, there are seven cards to work with at the outset. If the player is fortunate, one or more of these top cards will be aces. Aces are automatically moved to an area above the Tableau, where they serve as foundations for subsequent building. Given great luck, a two and a three of the same suit as the foundation ace may be showing. All such matching top cards are transferred to the area above the Tableau: Ace, two, three, etc., by suit. When the top card of any pack is moved, the card under it may be turned over. If this card also proves playable, the next card down may be turned face up, and so forth.

The other type of play involves moving cards about within the Tableau itself. In the case of the foundation aces, the order of building is ascending. Inside the Tableau, however, the order of sequences is always descending: King, queen, jack, ten, nine . . . two. Furthermore, a red card must always be placed on a black card, and vice versa. A variety of plays are possible. For example, if among the top cards there are a black king and a red queen, the latter can at once be moved and laid on the former. As a result of this switch,

the face-down card at the top of the pack from which the queen was
taken is now turned up.

Should it prove to be a black jack, it is played on the queen, and
the next card under the jack is turned up. Elsewhere among the top
cards may be a black eight and a red seven. The seven is shifted
over onto the eight. A red nine may now appear in the turning of
the top card from the seven's old pack. Should this happen, the black
eight with its attached red seven are both moved over onto the nine.
Should a black ten surface where the eight was, then the whole
nine-eight-seven chain is moved onto the ten. When all of the cards
in a pack are played off, leaving an empty space, a king can be moved
to fill the vacancy. Play proceeds within the Tableau in the above
manner. As opportunities arise, cards can be moved up to build on
the foundation aces. Such moves cannot be made from the middle of
a chain, however. The card to be moved must either be the last in
a building chain, or alone and face up at the top of a pack.

Frequently, a temporary impasse will occur in which no play seems
possible. At such times the player may resort to the stock of 24
cards previously set aside. The stock is thumbed through, three cards
at a time. The first group of three cards is turned face up as a
pack, and the top card is examined. If this card is playable, the
second card in the group may also be used. Similarly, the third card
is eligible for play if the second is played successfully. If the

first card in the three-card pack is not playable, the player turns
up the next pack of three. In this fashion, the player passes through
the entire stock. When all the way through the stock, repeat from
the beginning of the stock. Once a pass through is made without a
successful play resulting, the game automatically ends.

2. Double Solitaire:

Here there are two players, and each tries to play the entire deck
on foundation aces before his opponent. The play differs from Solitaire
in that the foundation aces are mutually held property. For instance,
if one player moves an ace of hearts above his/her Tableau line, the
other player may lay a two of heart on it, and so forth. A player
may delay playing cards on foundation aces to temporarily block certain
plays by the opponent. Should neither player play off all remaining
cards, the person with the fewest cards in his/her Tableau and stockpile
automatically becomes the winner.

Session wrap-up; enjoy a snack if desired.

Review the playing procedures and rules for Solitaire and Double
Solitaire to see if the elder has specific questions. Encourage the
elder to practice the game during the week (a short game of Double
Solitaire might be a fun way to begin the next session)!

ENDING THE SESSION:

Share the basket.

Talk about and confirm next session.

AFTER THE SESSION:

Write up comments.

IDEAS FOR MODIFYING THE ACTIVITY: Card decks with large print and
overside decks ar available from department stores and mail order
companies. Braille playing cards are also available. For those who
need assistance managing the cards, Hale (1981) suggests trying various
grooved holders, available from self-help equipment firms, or a tray
that hangs out of sight just below the table top. Battery-operated
card shufflers and automatic card dealers are also available and might
be helpful.

An effective card holder suggested by Hale (1981) can be made by sawing
slots 1 inch (2.5 cm) deep in a piece of solid wood that is at least
2 inches (5 cm) thick. "A piece of felt or pimple rubber glued to
the base will keep it from slipping" (Hale, 191, p. 342).

Possible resources to contact concerning these items include local hobby shops, discount stores, sporting goods stores, state commissions for the blind, and the National Foundation for the Blind, Inc. The occupational therapy department of a hospital is another good source. In addition, the local senior citizens center or parks and recreation department may be of assistance in locating these aids. (Check the resource list at the end of this unit for further assistance.)

TIPS FOR SAFETY: Make sure the elder is comfortably situated in the playing area and that it is well lighted.

UNIT NAME: Games

ACTIVITY PLAN 6: INDOOR GOLF

PURPOSE OF ACTIVITY: To involve the elder in a semi-active leisure sport, possibly reviving an old interest. If golf is not familiar, this activity will introduce a new leisure interest.

DESCRIPTION OF ACTIVITY: The leader will explain and demonstrate a variation of golf. The leader and elder will then participate in the game together.

BENEFITS OF ACTIVITY: Indoor golf is fun, and golf may be an activity in which the elder has previously participated, thus reviving an old interest. In addition, this game involves hand-eye coordination and very moderate physical activity; it gets the participant moving about. The activity is challenging and can be enjoyed individually or with others.

BEFORE THE SESSION:

   Things to do

The leader will prepare the equipment to be utilized, which includes collecting four shoe boxes of similar sizes. One end of the box is cut out so that the golf ball can be knocked into it. The lids are removed and boxes are placed side by side and upside down.

Points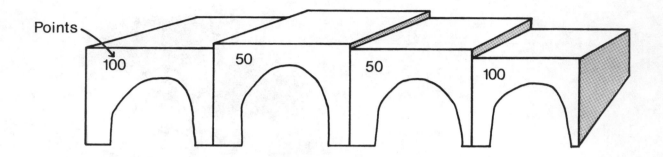

The different boxes are scored as indicated above; write the possible number of points over each box. Put masking tape over the tops of the four boxes so that they will remain side by side once play begins.

The leader is encouraged to practice Indoor Golf before presenting to the elder.

Things to take

The equipment described above
Golf club, preferably a putter
Three to five golf balls
Paper and pencils to keep score, if desired

WHAT TO DO DURING THE SESSION:

Greeting and opening chat; pay attention to any immediate needs.

Complete any unfinished business from previous session.

Explain the session's activities.

Do activities.

1. <u>Indoor Golf:</u>

To play this game, place the four shoe boxes on a noncarpeted floor such as the kitchen floor or a hardwood floor. If furniture or rugs need to be rearranged, do so only with permission of the elder. Carpeted floors can be used, but accuracy may be more difficult.

The first player (the leader should go first to demonstrate how the game is played) stands about 6 feet from the shoe boxes with a golf club and three to five golf balls. He/she knocks the balls, one at a time, toward the holes and scores as indicated. Keep score as desired and repeat as often as desired.

Session wrap-up; enjoy a snack if desired.

If furniture or rugs were rearranged for this activity, make sure they are returned to their original position.

ENDING THE SESSION:

Share the basket.

Talk about and confirm next session.

If possible, leave the equipment with the elder and encourage playing Indoor Golf during the week; see if he/she can achieve higher scores with practice!

AFTER THE SESSION:

Write up comments.

IDEAS FOR MODIFYING THE ACTIVITY: Some very light hand and arm stretching motions might be included as a warm-up.

The Indoor Golf game may be played from a seated position. A tennis or similar size ball may be used instead of a golf ball. The ball may also be rolled (as in bowling) rather than hit with the golf club. A bigger target and larger-size balls may be used for the visually impaired. An auditory signal, such as tapping on the target, may improve aim; a colorful target is also recommended.

TIPS FOR SAFETY: Make sure the playing area is free from objects that might prove hazardous and that it is well lighted. Provide for periods of rest as needed. If the participant has trouble stooping and/or bending to retrieve the balls, provide assistance as necessary.

UNIT NAME: Games

ACTIVITY PLAN 7: FINGER SHUFFLEBOARD

PURPOSE OF ACTIVITY: To involve the elder in a nonstrenuous competitive game.

DESCRIPTION OF ACTIVITY: The leader will explain how to play finger shuffleboard,* set up the playing area, and participate with the elder in as many games as desired.

BENEFITS OF ACTIVITY: This activity is ideal for individuals whose movements may be restricted. The activity requires little organization, few rules, little equipment, and limited activity. It does, however, exercise finger and arm muscles and involves hand-eye coordination.

This activity provides social stimulation and interaction with others, competition, and enjoyment. It is also a good activity to enjoy with other friends, grandchildren, etc.

BEFORE THE SESSION:

   Things to do

The leader might want to construct and paint a tabletop finger shuffleboard game. This is certainly not required but could be constructed if desired. Suggested dimensions are diagramed below:

*Adapted from R. C. Adams, A. N. Daniel, J. A. McCubbin, and L. Rullman, Games, sports and exercises for the physically handicapped. Copyright ©1982. Lea and Febiger. Used by permission.

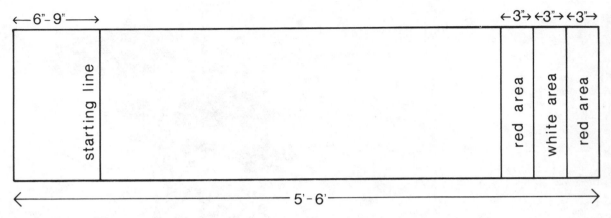

Plywood is recommended for the playing surface. Three coats of varnish are recommended to provide a good base for the sliding checker. If the leader anticipates playing doubles (four players), paint the scoring area on both ends of the board. The leader is encouraged to practice this game before presenting.

Things to take

Checkers
Masking tape (for marking playing surface)
Pen or Magic Marker to write on the masking tape
Paper and pencil to keep score

WHAT TO DO DURING THE SESSION:

Greeting and opening chat; pay attention to any immediate needs.

Complete any unfinished business from previous session.

Explain the session's activities.

After explaining the activity, check to determine where the game will be best arranged. A kitchen, dining, or card table is recommended. A kitchen counter could also be used.

Do activities.

The objective of the game is to propel checkers to the opposite end of the "court" while attempting to score points and prevent the opponent from scoring. The players stand or sit beside each other at one end of the table. Each player receives three checkers of one color (red or black). The player with red checkers starts the game. A checker is placed anywhere behind the starting line before propelling it to the opposite end of the table.

The players shoot alternately, first red, then black, then red, and so forth, until one round (six checkers) is completed. The checker

may be flicked or pushed across the table. The score is recorded
at the end of each round. The player with the most points at the
end of a round starts the next round. In case of a tie, the player
who scored the last point starts the next round.

Use masking tape to mark the table (see illustration). Make sure
the masking tape is firmly pressed to the table so that the checkers
will slide over it easily.

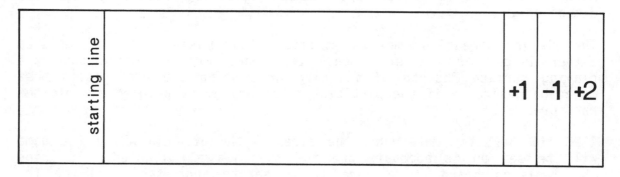

Scoring:

   There are three areas at one end of the table: +1 point area,
   -1 point area, and +2 area.

   A checker that hangs over the back edge of the +2 area is called
   a "hanger" and is worth 5 points.

   If a checker stops exactly between two scoring areas, no score
   is allowed. The checker must be more than halfway into a point
   area before a point count can be determined.

   Any checker that goes off the end or the side of the table is
   termed a "dead" checker.

   The first player who reaches 15 points it the winner.

   If there is a tie game at 15 points or more, play is continued
   in regular rounds until the tie is broken.

   Session wrap-up; enjoy a snack if desired.

ENDING THE SESSION:

   Share the basket.

   Talk about and confirm next session.

AFTER THE SESSION:

   Write up comments.

IDEAS FOR MODIFYING THE ACTIVITY: A large sheet of smooth paper, such as the kind often used to cover tables at banquets or covered-dish dinners, may be used as the playing surface. This paper would be marked with a pen or Magic Marker, according to the previously suggested dimensions.

The playing dimensions may be modified, thus making the playing area either larger or smaller. Small bean bags may be tossed onto the playing surface instead of flicking or pushing the checkers. These might be desirable if the participant has any joint problems in his/her hand or arm.

TIPS FOR SAFETY: Make sure the size of the area in which the game will be set up is adequate and the room is well lighted. If using the tabletop board, make sure it is secure and stable. Watch for signs of fatigue and allow for periods of rest or stop playing as indicated. It is a good idea to do some warm-up hand and finger exercises such as slowly opening and closing the hand.

REFERENCES AND RESOURCES

Activity director's guide. Published monthly by Eymann Publications, Inc., 1490 Huntington Circle, Box 3577, Reno, NV 89505.

Adams, R. C., Daniel, N., McCubbin, J. A., & Rullman, L. Games, sports and exercises for the physically handicapped (3rd ed.). Philadelphia: Lea & Febiger, 1982.

Biegal, L. The best year's catalogue: A source book for older Americans solving problems and living fully. New York, B. P. Putnam's Sons, 1978.

Fish, H. U. Activities programs for senior citizens. Old Tappan, NY: Parker, 1971.

Harbin, E. O. The fun encyclopedia. Nashville, TN: Abingdon Press, 1968.

Heaton, I. C., & Thorstenson, C. T. Planning for social recreation. Boston: Houghton Mifflin, 1978.

Hohenstein, M. Games for people of all ages. Minneapolis, MN: Bethany House, 1980.

Reader's Digest. Book of 1000 family games. Pleasantville, NY: The Reader's Digest Association, 1971.

Wiswell, P. I hate charades. New York: Sterling, 1982.

Adapted Activity Equipment[*]

One-handed Card Holder
For one-handed people to hold playing cards. This clamps to the edge of the table; plastic discs pinch together to hold cards.
Supplier: Fred Sammons, Inc.

Checker Set
For the visually limited or blind; board is marked with recessed 1-inch squares; checkers are round for one player and square for the other.
Supplier: American Foundation for the Blind

Dominoes
For the visually limited. Prominent raised dots identify the blocks.
Supplier: American Foundation for the Blind

Extra-Large Playing Cards
For those with limited sight or limited grasping strength.
Supplier: Cleo Living Aids

Standard Poker Playing Cards
Enlarged numerals for the visually impaired.
Supplier: Cleo Living Aids

Low-Vision Playing Cards
Suits are color-coded for players with low vision.
Supplier: American Foundation for the Blind

Hi-Marks
For creating raised surfaces to mark wood, cloth, paper, and metal.
Useful for adaptng games for easier identification.
Supplier: American Foundation for the Blind

Suppliers*

American Foundation for the Blind
Consumer Products Division
15 West 16th Street
New York, NY 10011

Cleo Living Aids
3957 Mayfield Rd.
Cleveland, OH 44121

Fred Sammons, Inc.
Box 32
Brookfield, IL 60513

*These and additional suggestions for adapted activity equipment are found in Hamill, C. M., & Oliver, R. C. Therapeutic activities for the handicapped elderly (Appendix B, pp. 261-265; Appendix E, pp. 275-278). Rockville, MD: Aspen Systems Corporation, 1980. Reprinted with permission of Aspen Publishers, Inc.

CHAPTER 8

Hobbies
Activity Plans

UNIT NAME: Hobbies

ACTIVITY PLAN 2: FUN WITH BOOKS (The first activity in all recreation units should be "Assessing Recreation Interests." See pages 55 to 57.)

PURPOSE OF ACTIVITY: To introduce a variety of activities involving books.

DESCRIPTION OF ACTIVITY: The leader will present information on a variety of activities involving books. These include collecting, reading (book reviewing), and participating in book clubs. Leader and elder will interact throughout the session.

BENEFITS OF ACTIVITY: Books can be an interesting hobby! Books appeal to a wide variety of interests. Activities involving books can provide educational experiences, sensory stimulation, and mental stimulation. These activities can expand one's interest and promote a feeling that one has participated in another's experiences.

BEFORE THE SESSION:

    Things to do

The leader should read over the information presented in this activity plan to become familiar with the activities to be discussed. A visit to the local public library is also recommended. Library employees can provide assistance and/or locate resources to pursue these interests locally. If the leader knows of someone who enjoys books as a hobby, contact this person for ideas and/or assistance.

Things to take

Any materials that support or illustrate the activities to be discussed, depending on their availability to the leader. No specific materials are required.

WHAT TO DO DURING THE SESSION:

Greeting and opening chat; pay attention to any immediate needs.

Complete any unfinished business from previous session.

Explain the session's activities.

The leader explains the purpose of this session and highlights the activities to be discussed.

Do activities.

1. Introduce the topic of book collecting:

Book collecting is an enjoyable hobby. Books can be collected according to the individual's circumstances, personality, and tastes. Book collecting can be a relatively inexpensive pursuit also. There are still many books to be "swapped" or bought at bargain ("garage sale") prices!

The elder should first decide if he/she enjoys the process of collecting. The elder then considers what type of book he/she is interested in collecting. It is a good idea to inventory the books the elder currently possesses. These might even be collected from different places in the house, cataloged, and rearranged if desired.

Some ideas for getting started on this hobby include writing to a few booksellers for catalogs, contacting local bookstores (possibly plan to visit), contact known book collectors to discuss their collections and receive guidance for starting a collection, visit a library, museum, or historical society where collections might be housed, contact the public library for assistance, and read the works of a few of the authorities on book collecting.

2. Discuss the pleasures of reading:

As in book collecting, the first thing the elder must decide is what does he/she want to read about? What interests him/her most? It is important to answer this question because the elder will be most motivated to read about topics of personal interest.

The local public library is an excellent source to tap for pursuing reading interests. Library assistants can help choose particular authors or titles or help locate materials on specific subjects. Records and magazines are also available. Most libraries include a collection of large-print books or magazines for one's consideration.

A growing program at libraries across the nation is outreach or home-delivered services. Some of these programs include a monthly or quarterly newsletter. Check with the local public library to see if this service is available.

"If the elder cannot read large print or is unable to hold a book and turn pages, he/she is probably eligible for Talking Books" (Lunt, 1982, p. 113). As Hale (1981) describes, the books are delivered by mail at no charge to the elder. In addition, a record player or tape recorder will also be loaned, without charge, if needed by the elder; special attachments may be requested. By applying for this service, the elder will receive a free subscription to <u>Talking Book Topics</u>. This magazine includes newly available books.

Book clubs are organized in many communities. These clubs promote a variety of activities and services, including book reviewing and book sharing. Once again, the local public library is an excellent place to inquire about the existence of a book club in one's community.

   Session wrap-up; enjoy a snack if desired.

Leader and elder should discuss their interest in pursuing one or more of the activities discussed during this session. The leader will help the elder determine how he/she would like to pursue these interests.

ENDING THE SESSION:

   Share the basket.

   Talk about and confirm next session.

The leader and elder will discuss a plan of action to contact resources and obtain follow up information prior to the next session.

AFTER THE SESSION:

   Write up comments.

IDEAS FOR MODIFYING THE ACTIVITY: Check with local bookstores and public libraries concerning the availability of large-print editions of books and magazines. Reference has already been made to the availability of Talking Books.

Various book holders, both commercially manufactured and homemade, are available. These include holders designed for lapboards, tables, and bed trays as well as free-standing or suspended book holders.

Various types of magnifying aids are also commercially available. These can be held by hand, placed directly over lines of print, suspended around the neck, or mounted on a stand. Prism glasses are available and help one to see things at right angles to the eyes when lying down. Hale (1981) suggested such glasses might also help to reduce eyestrain when neck motion is limited. Hale (1981) cautions, however, that these magnifying aids should never be used extensively without medical consultation.

"Use the eraser of a pencil, buy a rubber finger cover, or dip a finger into Tacky Fingers (available at stationery stores) to help turn pages" (Lunt, 1982, p. 114). "When the fingers cannot be used but there is good control of the arm, pages can be turned with the side of the hand or the elbow if a book or magazine is lying flat" (Hale, 1981, p. 30).

TIPS FOR SAFETY: Make sure the lighting is of adequate intensity and falls properly so that enough light is shed on the book (Hale, 1981).

No specific precautions are necessary other than sensitivity to the participant's general well-being. Watch for signs of tiring. Do not be too concerned with discussing all of the activities presented in this activity plan. Any activities not covered during this session can be discussed in later sessions.

UNIT NAME: Hobbies

ACTIVITY PLAN 3: FUN WITH PUZZLES

PURPOSE OF ACTIVITY: To stimulate an interest in working puzzles of various types.

DESCRIPTION OF ACTIVITY: The leader will present a variety of puzzle activities. The elder will then select one or more of these activities in which to participate.

BENEFITS OF ACTIVITY: Puzzles offer an intriguing form of individual fun, and can also be enjoyed with others. They require limited physical activity and yet promote hand-eye coordination. Puzzles are mentally stimulating, requiring alertness, observation, and a good memory. Various types of puzzles also enhance vocabulary.

BEFORE THE SESSION:

   Things to do

The leader should make a copy of the crossword puzzle grid. The leader will also select a jigsaw puzzle (or a variety of jigsaw puzzles if possible) to bring along to the session.

The leader should read over the information in the activity plan and become familiar with the activities. The elder may wish to enjoy these activities with another person prior to the session.

Things to take

Paper and pencils for elder and leader
Jigsaw puzzle(s)
Grid for the crossword puzzle
Dictionary (optional)

WHAT TO DO DURING THE SESSION:

Greeting and opening chat; pay attention to any immediate needs.

Complete any unfinished business from previous session.

Explain the session's activities.

The leader will introduce the idea of participating in various puzzle
activities as a hobby, perhaps reviewing some of the benefits of these
activities. The leader will then briefly describe the two puzzle
activities contained in this session and ask the elder to select one
in which he/she would like to participate. (The other activity can
be saved for another session.)

Do activities.

1. Crossword Puzzle

The first crossword puzzle was made up by Arthur Wynne, who edited
the puzzle page of the Sunday New York World. It was published on
December 21, 1913, in the Fun Section of the World and was an instant
success. Here's that first published crossword puzzle[*] (an enlarged
copy of the puzzle and answers for the puzzle may be found at the
end of this activity plan):

2-3	what bargain hunters enjoy	6-22	what we all should be
4-5	a written acknowledgment	4-26	a daydream
6-7	such and nothing more	2-11	a talon
10-11	a bird	19-28	a pigeon
14-15	opposed to less	F-7	part of your head
18-19	what this puzzle is	23-30	a river in Russia
22-23	an animal of prey	1-32	to govern
26-27	the close of day	33-34	an aromatic plant
28-29	to elude	N-8	a fist
30-31	the plural of is	24-31	to agree with
8-9	to cultivate	3-12	part of a ship
12-13	a bar of wood or iron	20-29	one
16-17	what artists learn to do	5-27	exchanging
20-21	fastened	9-25	to sink in mud
24-25	found on the seashore	13-21	a boy
10-18	the fiber of the goumuti palm		

[*]Taken from Millington, R. Crossword puzzles, their history and their
cult (pp. 12, 160). Nashville, TN: Thomas Nelson, 1974. Used by
permission.

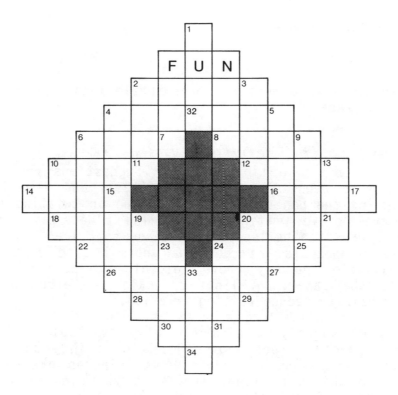

2. Jigsaw Puzzles

Jigsaw puzzles come in a variety of sizes, shapes, and designs and feature a variety of scenes. Puzzles with large, thick interlocking pieces may be most suitable for the participant. (While puzzles can be bought fairly inexpensively, they can also be "swapped" or borrowed. It's also possible to find puzzle bargains at local rummage sales.)

Session wrap-up; enjoy a snack if desired.

ENDING THE SESSION:

Share the basket.

Talk about and confirm next session.

During this time the leader will discuss the resources available for participating in puzzle activities. Possible resources for jigsaw puzzles have been discussed above. Various types of word puzzles can be located in daily newspapers and popular magazines. Also, booklets and magazines containing crossword and other types of letter and word puzzles are available in bookstores, discount stores, and public libraries. The leader may want to leave a crossword puzzle for the elder to work on prior to the next session.

AFTER THE SESSION:

   Write up comments.

The leader should make a note of those puzzle ideas in which the elder expresses an interest.

IDEAS FOR MODIFYING THE ACTIVITY: Various techniques may be tried to improve the elder's writing ability. Suggestions for the leader's consideration have been offered by Lunt (1982) and Hale (1981). For example, wrapping the pen or pencil with tape or twisting rubber bands around it may improve writing grasp. The elder may find felt-tip pens easier to use than ball-point pens, and soft lead may be preferred to hard lead in pencils. Larger than normal size pens and pencils are also available and may prove helpful. Clipboards may be used to help hold the paper. A light sprinkle of talcum powder across the paper may help to reduce writing friction.

Various types of magnifying aids are also available. These can be held by hand, placed directly over lines of print, suspended around the neck, or mounted on a stand. Prism glasses are available and help one to see things at right angles to the eyes when lying down. Hale (1981) suggested such glasses might also help to reduce eyestrain, too, when neck motion is limited. These magnifying aids, however, should never be recommended without medical consultation.

The leader may choose to write down the elder's responses; this decision should also be desired by the elder, however.

Large-print editions of many books and magazines are available, as well as puzzles with large interlocking pieces. Thicker puzzle pieces will be easier to grasp. The local senior citizens center, the public library, and/or the occupational/recreation therapy departments of local hospitals may be able to locate puzzles with handles attached to the pieces for easier manipulation. Puzzles with fewer pieces may also be best. The leader is encouraged to make sure the type of scene depicted by the puzzle is appropriate to the age and interest of the participant.

TIPS FOR SAFETY: Make sure lighting is adequate. Choose a work area that allows the elder to sit and write comfortably.

No specific precautions are necessary other than sensitivity to the elder's general well-being. This activity can be a source of frustration, especially in conjunction with failing memory, eyesight, and fine motor coordination. Therefore, watch for signs of frustration, confusion, and/or fatigue. Do not rush the activity; allow for periods of rest as desired.

2-3   what bargain hunters enjoy   16-17 what artists learn to do
4-5   a written acknowledgment   12-13 a bar of wood or iron
6-7   such and nothing more   3-12 part of a ship
F-7   part of your head   8-9   to cultivate
14-15 opposed to less   1-32 to govern
2-11 a talon   N-8   a fist
10-11 a bird

		F	U	N			

(crossword diagram)

F U N

1
2   3
4   32   5
6   7   8   9
10   11   12   13
14   15   16   17
18   19   20   21
22   23 24   25
26   33   27
28   29
30   31
34

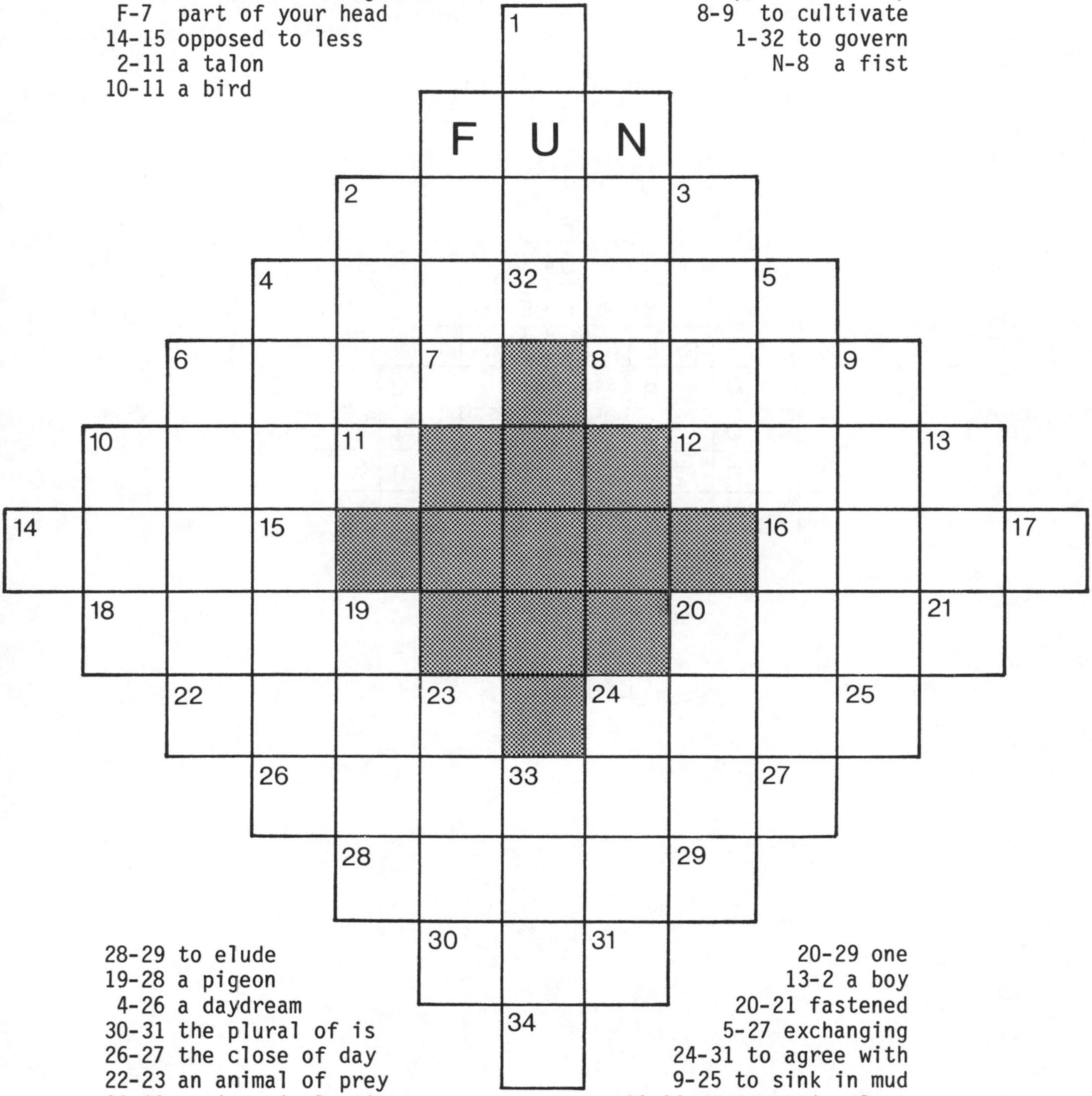

28-29 to elude   20-29 one
19-28 a pigeon   13-2 a boy
 4-26 a daydream   20-21 fastened
30-31 the plural of is   5-27 exchanging
26-27 the close of day   24-31 to agree with
22-23 an animal of prey   9-25 to sink in mud
23-30 a river in Russia   33-34 an aromatic plant
18-19 what this puzle is   24-25 found on the seashore
 6-22 what we all should be
10-18 the fiber of the goumuti palm

UNIT NAME: Hobbies

ACTIVITY PLAN 4: OUR FEATHERED FRIENDS

PURPOSE OF ACTIVITY: To provide suggestions for enjoying the hobby of bird watching.

DESCRIPTION OF ACTIVITY: The leader and elder will interact as the leader presents various ideas and suggestions for enjoying the hobby of bird watching. The elder will be encouraged to participate in various bird watching projects and activities and to think about other ways to get involved with this hobby.

BENEFITS OF ACTIVITY: Bird watching is an enjoyable and exciting hobby! Bird watching, study, and related activities provide stimulation for the senses and opportunities for new experiences. This hobby can be started and continued at home but also features opportunities for expanded interaction with others.

BEFORE THE SESSION:

   Things to do

The leader should read over the information presented in this activity plan to become familiar with the activities to be discussed. The leader may also consult some of the references listed at the end of the unit. If the leader knows of an avid bird-watcher or a community club for bird-watching enthusiasts, he/she may want to contact these resources for additional ideas, suggestions, and materials.

Things to take

WHAT TO DO DURING THE SESSION:

Greeting and opening chat; pay attention to any immediate needs.

Complete any unfinished business from previous session.

Explain the session's activities.

The leader introduces the topic of the session by stating that birds are one of the most easily studied groups in the animal kingdom. Birds can be observed any time of year, all around the world. Explain that various ideas and suggestions for pursuing this hobby will be discussed.

Do activities.

The participants will interact informally while discussing the following information:

Bird-watching basics include learning to identify birds and learning to find birds. Finding birds includes knowing where the particular bird is likely to be found, when to look for the bird, and how to observe the bird. These skills can be gained through study and practice.

Several excellent field guides are available to help identify birds. These can be obtained in bookstores or public libraries. In addition, 4-H extension or adult education extension programs often have free guides and pamphlets available, as do museums, wildlife refuges, and zoos.

With the help of a field guide, the leader and elder can try to identify the basic groups of birds likely to be found in the elder's area. They can also use the guide to help determine other unique field marks such as size, shape, bill, tail, coloration, and behavior. Additional information to pursue concerns what time of the year is best to observe certain birds. Although it varies, in general the spring (April to early June) and/or fall (September to late November) migration seasons tend to produce the greatest variety of birds at most locations.

Watching and listening to the seasonal migrations of birds is an exciting bird-watching activity. These migrations can often be observed as a part of the changing seasons. Again, field guides and related resources, particularly those pertaining to the elder's area, can be helpful in determining what types of birds to watch for and when migration occurs. The leader and elder might discuss past experiences of observing migrating flocks of birds. The elder may also express an interest in attracting birds to the home. Usually food, water, and/or birdhouses will attract birds. After determining what types

of birds are normally found in the area and which of these the elder
would like to attract, the appropriate kind of food can be provided.
The more variety offered, the more types of birds that might be
attracted.

Many species of birds nest in manmade birdhouses. Usually, the simpler
the birdhouse, the more successful it will be in attracting birds.
Brightly colored, elaborate houses are discouraged. In general, wood
is preferable to any other material used to build the birdhouse.

Hummingbirds can usually be attracted to one's home by hanging small
bottles or vials filled with one part sugar to three parts water.
It is preferable to color the sugar water solution red, as this will
attract the hummingbirds.

Collecting bird-related items may also be of interest to the elder.
Such activities might include collecting bird stamps, duck and other
decoys, wildlife art, autographs of famous bird-watchers, postcards
featuring paintings or photographs of birds, and embroidered shoulder
patches.

Session wrap-up; enjoy a snack if desired.

The leader and participant can discuss interest in pursuing one or
more of the activities discussed during this session.

ENDING THE SESSION:

Share the basket.

Talk about and confirm next session.

AFTER THE SESSION:

Write up comments.

It is a good idea for the leader to jot down those supplies or resources
(if any) that the participant will need to pursue specific bird-watching
interests.

IDEAS FOR MODIFYING THE ACTIVITY: No specific modifications are
indicated in this activity plan. These may be needed, however, after
a specific bird-watching activity is chosen. For example, learning
to recognize the songs and calls of birds may be an enjoyable way
for the visually impaired to identify birds; the use of binoculars
might also be of assistance in this activity.

TIPS FOR SAFETY: No special precautions are necessary for this session, other than sensitivity to the general well-being of the elder. There are many topics that could be discussed in this session; however, the leader should not insist that all topics be covered! Watch for signs of tiring, loss of attention, or confusion, and modify the length of the session accordingly.

UNIT NAME: Hobbies

ACTIVITY PLAN 5: ASTRONOMY

PURPOSE OF ACTIVITY: To stimulate an interest in astronomy by discussing a few facts about this subject and some ideas for making astronomical observations.

DESCRIPTION OF ACTIVITY: The leader will discuss a few facts about astronomy and highlight activities that can be engaged in by the "amateur astronomer." Information concerning the sun, moon, planets, and stars will be briefly presented.

BENEFITS OF ACTIVITY: Astronomy is an exciting subject, and does not necessarily require sophisticated equipment to enjoy. Astronomy, the study of the heavens, provides intellectual and sensory stimulation and can lead to participation in a variety of activities. This challenging hobby can be started and continued at home but also provides opportunities to interact with others.

BEFORE THE SESSION:

   Things to do

The leader should read over the information presented in this activity plan to become familiar with the areas to be discussed. He/she might also practice some of the activities presented. The leader may consult some of the references listed at the end of the unit. If the leader knows of an avid astronomer and/or a community astronomical society, these resources may be contacted for additional ideas, suggestions, and materials.

Things to take

Paper and pencil, and any information to be discussed, depending on its availability to the leader

WHAT TO DO DURING THE SESSION:

Greeting and opening chat; pay attention to any immediate needs.

Complete any unfinished business from previous session.

Explain the session's activities.

The leader briefly explains that various facts about astronomy will be discussed as well as ideas and suggestions for participation in this hobby.

Do activities.

Initial conversation between the leader and elder should attempt to get an idea of the elder's knowledge of and interest in astronomy. The following facts are presented as a way to stimulate conversation. The leader should not feel "on the spot" to know or learn these facts, however; they may be read from the activity plan.

1. Discuss interesting facts about the sun, such as:

    The sun's diameter is 865,000 miles; 109 times that of earth.
    The sun is made up entirely of gas kept together by gravity.
    The sun is almost 90 million miles away from the earth, and yet it is the nearest star to the earth.

2. Suggested activities:

    Allow sunlight to shine on a prism glass, projecting onto a piece of white paper. This produces a bright rainbow. Do not try to look at the sun through the prism glass!
    The time between when the sun rises in the east and sets in the west is called a solar day. Try to follow the sun's path during one solar day, noticing its location at sunrise, midday, and sunset; perhaps record the time of sunrise and sunset. However, never look straight at the sun while observing it, especially if using binoculars or a telescope; this will result in eye damage.

3. Explain some interesting facts about stars, such as:

    Stars are bodies shining by their own light.
    Many stars are larger than the sun.
    Stars are a vast distance from earth, even though they look like small fixed points of light.
    About 1,500 stars are visible at night without a telescope.

Early man looked at the stars and saw shapes and patterns. These star patterns are called constellations.

4. Other suggested activities dealing with the stars:

Pick out a few stars that look as though they are arranged in some kind of pattern--choose a group that's easy to recognize. Look for this group each night and observe it moving across the sky. This is due to the earth's rotation. Stars move as a whole, always keeping their same relative positions in the sky.
Locate the Pole Star or Polaris. This is a very bright star near the North Pole. Look northward to locate it.
Using a star map, try locating some of the various constellations.

5. Discuss interesting facts about the moon, such as:

The moon is just over one-fourth the diameter of the earth.
The moon has very low gravity; thus, the moon has no atmosphere.
On the average, the moon is 240,000 miles from the earth.
The moon shines only because it reflects the light of the sun.
The moon is the brightest object in the night sky.

6. Suggested activities dealing with the moon:

Look for the surface markings on the moon. These markings remind some of a human face--thus, the "Man in the Moon." These markings on the moon's surface are actually its seas, mountains, and craters. Try to observe the different phases of the moon; set aside a time each night to look at the moon. The moon revolves around the earth about once a month.

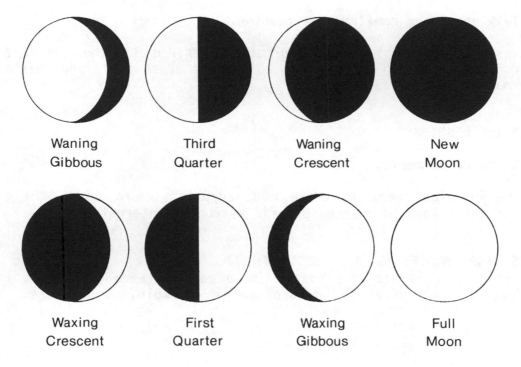

Waning   Third   Waning   New
Gibbous   Quarter   Crescent   Moon

Waxing   First   Waxing   Full
Crescent   Quarter   Gibbous   Moon

7. Discuss interesting facts about the planets, such as:

    The planets are sometimes called "wandering stars." They look
    like bright stars but change their positions in the constellations,
    and reflect the sun's light rather than emitting their own.
    There are nine major planets: Mercury, Venus, Earth, Mars, Jupiter,
    Saturn, Uranus, Neptune, Pluto. Mercury is the closest to the
    sun; Pluto is the farthest from the sun. Jupiter is the largest
    in diameter; Pluto is the smallest.
    Five planets--Mercury, Venus, Mars, Jupiter, and Saturn--are visible
    to the naked eye. Mercury is the most difficult of these five
    to see, however.
    Venus is the most brilliant object in our sky aside from the sun
    and the moon.

8. Suggested activity with planets:

    Using a star map or similar guide, try to locate various planets.
    It might be fun to discuss the advances in space travel that have
    occurred through the elder's lifetime.

    Session wrap-up; enjoy a snack if desired.

Leader and elder discuss their interest in pursuing one or more of
the activities presented during this session. The leader will help
the elder determine how he/she would like to pursue these interests.

ENDING THE SESSION:

   Share the basket.

   Talk about and confirm next session.

Discuss specific follow-up information desired by the participant.
Determine responsibilities for contacting resources and gathering
information if desired.

AFTER THE SESSION:

   Write up comments.

The leader might want to write down supplies or resources the elder
will need (if any) to pursue specific astronomy interests.

IDEAS FOR MODIFYING THE SESSION: No specific modifications are
indicated in this activity plan. These may be needed, however, after
a specific activity is chosen. For example, binoculars, even

inexpensive ones, will be helpful in observing the stars, moon, and planets. Planning to conduct this session at night may make observations possible during the session.

TIPS FOR SAFETY: No special precautions are necessary for this visit, other than sensitivity to the general well-being of the elder. Watch for signs of tiring, loss of attention, or confusion, and modify the length of the session accordingly. Remember: Never observe the sun directly, as this will damage the eyes.

UNIT NAME: Hobbies

ACTIVITY PLAN 6: INDOOR GARDENING

PURPOSE OF ACTIVITY: To show how an interest in gardening can be successfully pursued indoors.

DESCRIPTION OF ACTIVITY: The leader will present easy and inexpensive ideas for starting and maintaining an indoor garden. The leader and elder may wish to pot or repot a plant.

BENEFITS OF ACTIVITY: Working with plants is an enriching experience and is available to the elder whether he/she has a large home or apartment or one small window without much sun. In addition, gardening provides opportunities for mental and sensory stimulation, social interaction, and mild physical exercise. The participant can gain a sense of accomplishment and experience the opportunity to care for and about another living entity.

BEFORE THE SESSION:

   Things to do

The leader should read over the information presented in this activity plan to become familiar with the techniques to be discussed. The leader may also consult some of the gardening references listed at the end of the unit. The Reader's Digest Book, <u>Crafts and Hobbies</u>, is especially helpful and some of the information provided in this session plan is adapted from the section on indoor gardening. There are many catalogs and magazines with descriptions and instructions to gardeners, as well as many books on the subject. In addition, most newspapers feature a garden section. Florists and commercial greenhouses may be able to provide the leader with various resources and tips regarding growing houseplants. If the leader has a personal indoor garden or knows of others who do, he/she may gather additional ideas and suggestions. The leader may even be able to bring a stem or leaf cutting(s) for planting.

Things to take

Various resource materials that have been gathered by the leader
Paper and pencil for writing down any materials needed by the elder to pursue this activity
A variety of plant containers, depending on their availability to the leader
Some suitable soil or potting mix for potting or repotting
A small plant or plant cutting
Newspapers or other suitable material to protect work space
Basic planting tools (a kitchen fork or spoon will work just fine)
Any other materials needed to pursue additional suggested activities if the leader desires

WHAT TO DO DURING THE SESSION:

Greeting and opening chat; pay attention to any immediate needs.

Complete any unfinished business from previous session.

Explain the session's activities.

As the leader explains the session, it is a good idea to determine the elder's past and present experience with and interest in indoor gardening.

Do activities.

Introduce the idea of an indoor garden by discussing the various gardening possibilities, and then pursue related activities as desired. Gardening can range from simple to complex. It might involve a single plant, a window box, a terrarium, and possibly planting and upkeep of flowers outside the elder's home.

Plants need soil or potting mix, water, nutrients, warmth, moisture, and light to grow. Requirements for these essentials may vary somewhat, but are usually similar for most houseplants. In indoor gardening artificial light can supplement or substitute for sunlight. At this point it is a good idea to stop and ask the elder to make a list of supplies, such as potting mix, peat moss, sand, or tools he/she has on hand. If the budget allows and if desired, plans may be made to purchase needed supplies for the elder prior to the next session.

1. Plant containers and watering

Plant containers come in many varieties, such as wooden boxes, straw baskets, hanging containers, plastic pots, glazed ceramic pots, unglazed clay pots. Unglazed clay pots are recommended for indoor gardeners who sometimes overwater their plants, as water evaporates easily through the porous pottery. Plastic pots, however, are lighter, easier to clean, and more durable. Since water does not evaporate as easily in plastic, plants in these pots should be watered less frequently. Ceramic pots usually have no drain holes, thus plants in these pots need even less watering than those in plastic pots. Discuss these factors with the elder and help him/her select some appropriate and/or available containers.

A general recommendation is to water all houseplants thoroughly and infrequently, rather than frequently giving them small amounts of water. The need will differ, however, according to the plant, the container, the potting mix, the location, and the the air in the room. A rule of thumb--except for cacti--is that the soil should stay moist but not wet. Water at room temperature should be used to avoid shocking plants. At this point the leader and elder can inventory plants the elder has on hand and discuss the watering schedule he/she usually follows. The idea of keeping a written log of plant care activities may be discussed. This log would help the elder to remember when he/she had watered, repotted, and/or fertilized his/her plant collection.

2. Potting and repotting

Ready-made potting mixes are generally available. Since nutrients in these potting mixes are normally used up by the plants fairly quickly, adding plant food during the growing season may be necessary to keep the plants healthy. Commercial plant foods come in tablet, powder, and liquid forms; follow instructions on the container.

3. Plant reproduction

This involves cutting off a part of a plant, usually a stem or leaf, and planting the cutting. The cutting should be planted in a moist rooting mix and kept in a warm, humid, and bright (but not sunny) place until roots form. (Soft stems will root in water any time of year.) The elder may have some plants that have grown too large, or may simply want to multiply some plants he/she likes. If so, choose one of the above methods and try reproducing the plants.

4. Terrariums

A terrarium made of untinted glass or plastic is recommended. It should not leak and should not be placed in direct sunlight. Ferns, lichens, and mosses are ideal plants to use in a terrarium. Ask the elder if he/she has an interest in starting a terrarium.

To make a terrarium use a clear glass container with a lid. (The large glass jars used by commercial users of food are ideal.) Place a ½-inch or so layer of pebbles in the bottom for drainage, and then put in about 4 inches of soil. Small pieces of charcoal added to the soil will help keep the terrarium clear. Dig holes for plants, spread roots, and pack soil firmly around plants. Put the lid on the container and place the terrarium in a light area--but not in direct sunlight. If glass becomes cloudy, remove the lid and replace it again when sides are clear.

Session wrap-up; enjoy a snack if desired.

ENDING THE SESSION:

Share the basket.

Talk about and confirm next session.

To help the participant decide how he/she would like to pursue this interest, consider how much time he/she would like to devote to gardening. Some plants, such as terrariums or bottle gardens, require little upkeep. Other plants, such as cacti, may require more upkeep but only at certain times of the year. All-season bulbs and window boxes of flowering plants, however, will require frequent care throughout the year, as will food crops such as beans and mushrooms. The greater the variety of plants, the more continuous interest they can provide (Hale, 1981).

The leader and elder will make specific plans (if desired) to contact resources and obtain follow-up information on needed supplies prior to the next visit. This will hopefully be a shared responsibility, but the leader may have to take charge in making these contacts and gathering supplies.

Many public television stations feature periodic garden segments that the elder can plan to view on a regular basis.

AFTER THE SESSION:

Write up comments.

It is a good idea for the leader to jot down supplies and tools the elder will need (if any) to pursue gardening interests.

IDEAS FOR MODIFYING THE SESSION: Most of the activities involved in indoor gardening can be carried out while sitting at a table. Lightweight plastic pots are available and even soilless composts for individuals with certain allergies.

Old kitchen forks and spoons can be used as tools. If tools are purchased, a set of miniature tools might be considered (Hale, 1981). They will be lighter and easier to handle. The handles of tools may also be built up to make them easier to grasp.

Plants should always be within easy reach. Large plants in pots too heavy to move and pots on high shelves and/or hanging baskets are not recommended. A tabletop garden gives the opportunity to grow and display a variety of plants and provides clearance for the gardener using a wheelchair (Hunt, 1981).

To cut down on the need to move frequently from place to place, or often get up and down, wear an apron with pockets to carry supplies and tools. A child's coaster wagon, or some type of roll cart/caddy may also prove helpful for transporting and storing needed supplies (Lunt, 1982).

TIPS FOR SAFETY: It is important that the work space is comfortable and that proper lighting is available. Monitor the use of tools and make sure the work area, particularly the floor, is cleaned properly at the end of the vist. Make sure that all materials and supplies are properly stored.

Prior to beginning the session activities, question the elder concerning any known allergies to the materials he/she may be handling. The leader may also refer to available medical information. Indicated precautions should be observed.

Observe the elder for signs of fatigue, confusion, or distraction. Take time to discuss various aspects of the session as the elder desires, even if all topics are not covered; these can be covered during later sessions.

UNIT NAME: Hobbies

ACTIVITY PLAN 7: MUSIC APPRECIATION

PURPOSE OF ACTIVITY: To demonstrate that persons with little musical background or ability can enjoy listening to music for pleasure, relaxation, and study. This session will encourage an increased interest in music.

DESCRIPTION OF ACTIVITY: During this session, the leader will gather information concerning playing abilities and interests, listening experiences, and music preferences of the participant. He/she will then discuss with the elder various ways to appreciate and enjoy music. Actual participation in a music appreciation activity is included.

BENEFITS OF ACTIVITY: No form of recreation gets such a universal response as music. The response one makes to music can be physical, emotional, intellectual, social, or spiritual, or a combination of these. In addition, music activities can provide accompaniment for exercise, opportunities for creative expression, relief of self-concern, and stimulation of memory through an old favorite song.

BEFORE THE SESSION:

   Things to do

The leader should become familiar with the information to be discussed. He/she is also encouraged to determine additional ways the elder could appreciate and enjoy music. The leader can ask questions from this activity plan during any previous session. This helps in selecting music to include during this session.

Things to take

Paper and pencil
Phonograph or tape player
Variety of records or cassette tapes

WHAT TO DO DURING THE SESSION:

Greeting and opening chat; pay attention to any immediate needs.

Complete any unfinished business from previous session.

Explain the session's activities.

The leader briefly explains the purpose of this session and highlights some of the topics to be discussed.

Do activities.

To begin, the leader asks questions about the elder's music abilities and interests. Some questions which could be used for this purpose are listed at the end of this activity plan. When appropriate, the leader reacts to the elder's comments by discussing various ideas for pursuing interests. For example, if the elder stated he/she enjoyed listening to a variety of records or tapes, the leader could suggest the possibility of joining a music appreciation club whose members exchange records or tapes. During this discussion allow time for reminiscing--in fact, encourage it as much as possible. Also, be sure to make note of comments that might give an indication of the elder's musical background, personal preferences, abilities, and limitations.

The following ideas for appreciating and enjoying music can be discussed. Again, be sure to note those ideas that spark an interest, and provide time for interacting and reminiscing.

1. Learn to play an instrument such as an autoharp or portable chord organ. (Local musicians or music educators are often helpful in planning and teaching.)

2. Join a music appreciation club. Discussion groups develop from the club, and members may even do research in the library on musical topics of their choice. Members also often go to concerts together. (Many senior citizens centers have a music club.)

3. Attend educational sessions of a musical nature such as pre-concert lectures about coming muscial programs. If attendance is not possible, perhaps listen to a tape of the lecture.

4. Read about music, composers, and musicians.

5. View or listen to musical programs, such as opera, ballet, drama,
    etc., often featured on public television channels or radio
    stations.

6. Listen to music. There are many approaches to listening to music:

    If information about the music is available, read it before
    listening to the music; this provides interesting insight into
    the music's background and composition.
    Focus on the story the music is telling or the scene it's
    describing.
    Focus on characteristics of the music, such as the rhythm and
    tempo.
    Discuss feelings and/or memories the music evokes.
    Participate in a "name that tune" type of activity.
    Reseach the history of the composer and the period in which the
    music was written or popular.
    Simply relax and enjoy the music.
    Read or write poetry to the music.

7. Visit the public library. Most library collections usually include
    records and/or tapes for listening purposes.

8. Attend musical programs featured in the community. Watch church
    and school calendars for free programs, especially during the
    holiday seasons. Music teachers are often glad to have an audience
    for their student recitals, and in college communities, faculty
    and student concerts provide opportunities to hear quality music
    inexpensively (often free). Check the community schedule for
    "artist in the park" types of performances. Adult education and
    college extension departments are additional resources.

9. Use music as a background for other activities.

The above ideas should be discussed with various characteristics of
the elder's in mind. These include such things as previous background,
experience, exposure to music, cultural and ethnic characteristics,
abilities and limitations, and the elder's interests and needs in
the realm of music. Be receptive to ideas suggested by the elder
and feel free to suggest additional ideas not listed above.

If time permits and/or if desired, the leader and elder may participate
in a music appreciation activity. A suggested activity idea is to
play portions of a variety of musical selections and ask the elder
to "name that tune." Allow time for interacting and reminiscing.
Occasionally, spend a few additional minutes listening to a song and
asking the elder related questions such as:

    Can you describe the feelings the singer is trying to express?
    What is the mood created by the music and/or voice?
    What types of songs are your favorites?
    Do you associate any particular event with this song?

10. Discuss Recordings for Recovery. This is a philanthropic volunteer
     organization which provides tapes to hospitals, nursing homes,
     home-centered individuals, and the like.   All types of tapes
     are available, including a wide variety of music.   Tapes may
     be custom made to fit specific needs.   For details, write to:
     Recordings for Recovery, Box 288, Oakmont, PA 15139.

     Session wrap-up; enjoy a snack if desired.

Discuss the ideas that appealed to the elder and discuss plans for
pursuing desired interests.

ENDING THE SESSION:

     Share the basket.

     Talk about and confirm next session.

Discuss specific follow-up information desired by the elder.   Determine
responsibilities for contacting resources and gathering information.

AFTER THE SESSION:

     Write up comments.

Look over the written information gathered during the session and
make necessary additions or clarifications.

IDEAS FOR MODIFYING THE ACTIVITY: Hale (1981) points out that
individuals with limited hand or arm control may find supporting their
forearms with shoulder slings helps when playing keyboard instruments;
mouthsticks might also be used to strike the keys.   The elder may
find the organ easier to play than the piano since organ keys require
a pressing rather than a striking motion.

If the elder does not own a record player or tape player and cannot
afford one, these are usually available on a check-out basis from
the public library; records and cassettes are also available.   Other
organizations, such as the National Library Service for the Blind
and Physically Handicapped, Library of Congress, Washington, DC 20542,
provide similar services.   Of special interest are braille music scores
and records and tape recordings on musical history available from
the National Library Service for the Blind and Physically Handicapped.
This organization has also developed a system using vibrating boards,
tone boxes, and percussion instruments to enable hearing-impaired
individuals to perceive and appreciate musical rhythms (Hale, 1981).

The radio provides a good way to enjoy music and may be used as an alternative to a phonograph or tape player. Time can be spent helping the elder select the desired stations. Extra time may also be taken to familiarize the elder with public television channels and available musical program offerings.

Phonograph turntables often have automatic cueing devices for easier operation. It may also be possible to attach devices which control lowering and lifting of the pick-up (Hale, 1981). Still, if hand or arm coordination is limited, cassettes may be easier to manage (Hale, 1981). The occupational therapy department of the local hospital is an excellent source to tap concerning other aids or assistive devices.

Controls, earphone receivers, and other devices that connect to TV/radio extension outlets are commercially available. These may enhance listening capabilities.

Special receivers may be required to listen to radio reading services for the blind and physically disabled. For a listing of these radio services, direct requests to the National Library Service for the Blind and Physically Handicapped, Library of Congress, Washington, DC 20542.

TIPS FOR SAFETY: No special precautions are necessary for this session other than sensitivity to the general well-being of the elder. There are many topics to be discussed in this session, so the leader should not insist that all topics be covered. Watch for signs of tiring, loss of attention, or confusion, and modify the length of the activity accordingly.

POSSIBLE DISCUSSION QUESTIONS FOR MUSIC APPRECIATION

Performance skills

1. Do you now or have you ever participated in music activities such as singing in a choir or chorus or playing in a band or orchestra?

2. What types of musical instruments do you play, if any?

3. Have you ever studied singing or playing musical instruments? Would this be a future interest of yours?

4. How well can you read music? If not at all, would you like to learn to read music?

Listening experiences

1. How often do you listen to the radio?

2. If you own a record player, how often do you use it?

3. Do you have a record collection?

4. How often do you attend musical programs that might be sponsored by various groups in your community? Would you like to attend more musical programs in the future?

5. What types of musical programs would you like to attend (opera, solo recitals, symphony programs, etc.)?

6. Do you ever read books, magazine articles, or reviews about music?

Music preferences

1. What types of music do you like best (popular, jazz, soul, classical, country, etc.)?

2. What are your favorite types of performing groups (orchestras, choirs, soloists, marching bands, dance bands, etc.)?

IS THERE ANYTHING ELSE YOU WOULD LIKE TO DISCUSS ABOUT YOUR MUSIC INTERESTS AND ABILITIES?

REFERENCES AND RESOURCES

Batcheller, J. M., & Monsour, S. Music in recreation and leisure. Dubuque, IA: Wm. C. Brown, 1983.

Beard, T. F. How to find your family roots. New York: McGraw-Hill, 1977.

Coffey, E. S. Your own book of nature and garden fun. New York: Hearthside Press, 1957.

Croom, E. A. Unpuzzling your past: A basic guide to genealogy. White Hall: Betterway Publications, 1983.

Cruickshank, A. D., & Cruickshank, H. G. 1001 questions answered about birds. New York: Dodd, Mead, 1958.

Gardening for handicapped and elderly persons. Washington, DC: Library of Congress.

Hale, G. The source book for the disabled. New York: Bantam, 1981.

Heimberg, M. M. Discover your roots: A new, easy guide for tracing your family tree. San Diego, CA: Communication Creativity, 1977.

Heintzelman, D. S. The birdwatcher's activity book. Harrisburg, PA: Stackpole Books, 1983.

Helmbold, F. W. Tracing your ancestry. Birmingham, England: Oxmoor House, 1976. (Contains good bibliographies)

Heriteau, J. Small fruit and vegetable gardens; a step-by-step guide: You do have enough space. New York: Popular Library, 1975.

Hobbies. Lightner Publishing Co., 1006 South Michigan Avenue, Chicago, Illinois. (Monthly subscriptions available)

Ichis, M. Handicrafts and hobbies for recreation and retirement. New York: Dodd, Mead, 1960.

Kohl, H. A book of puzzlements, play, and invention with language. New York: Schocken Books, 1981.

Levitt, I. M., & Marshall, R. K. Star maps for beginners. New York: Simon & Schuster, 1980.

Lunt, S. A handbook for the disabled: Ideas and inventions for easier living. New York: Charles Scribner, 1982.

Millington, R. Crossword puzzles, their history and their cult. Nashville, TN: Thomas Nelson, 1974.

Moore, P. Amateur astronomy. New York: W. W. Norton, 1968.

Muirden, J. Astronomy for amateurs. London: Cassell, 1969.

Reader's Digest. Crafts and hobbies. Pleasantville, NY: The Reader's Digest Association, 1979.

Ronan, C. A. The practical astronomer. New York: Macmillan, 1981.

Salny, R. W. Hobby collections A-Z. New York: Thomas V. Crowell, 1965.

Sidjwick, J. B. Observational astronomy for amateurs (4th ed.). Hillside, NJ: Enslow Publications, 1982.

Silberstein-Storfer, M. Doing art together. New York: Simon & Schuster, 1982.

Superintendent of Documents, U.S. Government Printing Office, Washington, DC. Write requesting to be placed on the mailing list of new publications. Many inexpensive pamphlets are frequently offered concerning hobbies.

World almanac. New York: New York World-Telegram and Sun. Revised annually. Check index for specific items. Note particularly the section "Art Galleries, Museums, and Historic Sites," and the section "Associations and Societies," which lists some major collector societies.

Adapted Activity Equipment[*]

Flower Gatherer
For those who are limited in reach or who can utilize only one hand. A strong, light tool for cutting and gathering flowers. Flat, gripping jaws hold the stem of a cut piece until released.
Supplier: Maddak, Inc.

Weed Puller
For those limited in bending or kneeling; can be used with one hand. A trigger-operated hand grip closes the jaw when squeezed.
Supplier: Maddak, Inc.
         6 Industrial Road
         Pequannock, NJ 07440

[*]These and additional suggestions for adapted activity equipment are found in Hamill, C. M., & Oliver, R. C. Therapeutic activities for the handicapped elderly (Appendix B, pp. 261-265). Rockville, MD: Aspen Systems Corporation, 1980. Reprinted with permission of Aspen Publishers, Inc.

CHAPTER 9

Literature Activity Plans

UNIT NAME: Literature

ACTIVITY PLAN 2: LETTER WRITING (The first activity in all recreation units should be "Assessing Recreation Interests." See pages 55 to 57.)

PURPOSE OF ACTIVITY: To present an activity that will serve as an introduction for writing poetry in later sessions.

DESCRIPTION OF ACTIVITY: The elder will write (or dictate) a letter to an individual of his/her choice. The leader will assist as needed.

BENEFITS OF ACTIVITY: Writing a letter is one method for encouraging the writing of poetry. Letter writing also requires some physical skills such as hand-eye coordination and small muscle use. Letter writing provides an opportunity for individual expression and can lessen feelings of isolation and/or detachment.

BEFORE THE SESSION:

    Things to do

    Things to take

Paper, pen or pencil, envelope, stamp
Recent newspaper or news magazine such as <u>Time</u>, <u>Newsweek</u>

WHAT TO DO DURING THE SESSION:

Greeting and opening chat; pay attention to any immediate needs.

Complete any unfinished business from previous session.

Explain the session's activities.

The leader explains that this session will focus on writing a letter. Prompt the elder to begin thinking of someone to whom he/she would like to write a letter.

Do activities.

Ask the elder to identify a person to whom he/she would like to write a letter. The leader might also write a letter during this session.

The elder will write a letter and prepare an envelope, with assistance as needed. The elder might like to read this letter to the leader or might prefer to keep it private; this desire for privacy should be respected. After the letter is written, discuss plans to mail the letter if desired. This would be a good time to discuss when and where mail is delivered to the house and find out if the elder is having any problems receiving or sending mail.

If the elder cannot or prefers not to write a letter to an individual, select a current event or a news or feature item from a newspaper or magazine. The elder can write a response to this article using a "letter to the editor" format.

The elder might also consider writing a "thank you" or appreciation letter to some special person or community agency. In addition, other individuals may be identified through home-centered services, nursing homes, hospitals, prisons, or foreign pen-pal services, who might like to receive mail.

Session wrap-up; enjoy a snack if desired.

This session may revive an interest in writing letters and a desire to keep in touch with certain individuals. The leader should assist the elder in this effort as needed.

ENDING THE SESSION:

Share the basket.

Talk about and confirm next session.

AFTER THE SESSION:

Write up comments.

IDEAS FOR MODIFYING THE ACTIVITY: Various techniques may be tried to improve the elder's writing ability. Suggestions for the leader's consideration have been offered by Lunt (1982) and Hale (1981). For example, wrapping the pen or pencil with tape or twisting rubber bands around it may improve writing grasp. The elder may find felt-tip pens easier to use than ball-point pens, and soft lead may be preferred to hard lead in pencils. Larger than normal size pens and pencils are also available and may prove helpful. Clipboards may be used to help hold the paper. A light sprinkle of talcum powder across the paper may help to reduce writing friction.

Various types of magnifying aids are also available. However, these aids should not be recommended without medical consultation.

Instead of writing a letter, consider taping it. It will be just as meaningful for someone to hear the voice as to receive a letter.

TIPS FOR SAFETY: Make sure lighting is adequate. Choose a work area that allows the elder to sit and write comfortably.

Do not rush this activity; allow for periods of rest as desired.

UNIT NAME: Literature

ACTIVITY PLAN 3: POETRY GEMS

PURPOSE OF ACTIVITY: To present an easy and enjoyable way to begin writing poetry.

DESCRIPTION OF ACTIVITY: The leader and elder will write poetry together. The poetry is arranged in a diamond shape, thus the title Poetry Gems.

BENEFITS OF ACTIVITY: People are pleased to see their thoughts arranged in a poetic form. This activity also stimulates the mind, provides an emotional outlet, and encourages talking and interacting.

BEFORE THE SESSION:

> **Things to do**

> **Things to take**

Paper, pen or pencil

WHAT TO DO DURING THE SESSION:

> **Greeting and opening chat; pay attention to any immediate needs.**

> **Complete any unfinished business from previous session.**

Explain the session's activities.

The leader explains that he/she and the elder are going to try their hand at writing poetry. They will start with a form in which words are arranged in a diamond shape. Other methods will be tried if desired. The poems included in the following section are reprinted by permission of Bi-Folkal Productions Inc., © 1983 Bi-Folkal Productions, Inc.; Madison, WI (Insight, 1983).

Do activities.

To begin, discuss a possible topic to write about. Another idea is to suggest a sentence "starter" such as "Fall reminds me of . . . .," "My favorite things about picnics are . . . .," "When I think of friendship, I think of . . . ."

Once the topic is selected, both leader and elder take turns suggesting a word describing the topic until eight words are compiled. For example, if the topic is fall, these words might be suggested: crisp, cool, changing, red, orange, gold, sad, sweet. These words would then be arranged in this way: The topic (fall) on the first line, two words on the second line, three words on the third line, two words on the fourth line, and one word on the fifth line. Thus,

                              fall

              cool   changing

      red   orange   gold

              sad   sweet

                             crisp

Once the leader and elder have tried this together a few times, encourage the elder to write a poem of this type on his/her own.

Another way to write poetry may also be tried. Simply begin discussing a topic, such as fall memories. During the discussion the leader writes down what the elder is saying. Then simply arrange the words in any shape that looks like poetry. Here are some examples:

    I remember when I was a boy
        I raked leaves one fall
        for a woman who was 97.
    October always reminds me
        of my friendship
        with that very beautiful woman.

            (and)

Every fall
     I got out my knitting needles.
I knitted
     socks and scarves and mittens
     for everyone in my family.

One fall
     my father punished me
     unjustly, I thought.
So I unraveled the scarf
     I was knitting for him.

               (and)

I like
     cool breezes
     crisp air
     birds hurrying south
     colored leaves, overhead and underfoot
     pumpkins
     first frost
     Halloween
     football
     fall.

Be sure to record and save the poems. These poems can be shared with others, saved in scrapbooks, or featured in newsletters.

Session wrap-up; enjoy a snack if desired.

The leader and elder can discuss plans to save and/or share the poems. Encourage the elder to write more poetry between sessions and begin a collection. Reading and sharing the poetry can be a part of future sessions. A poem could be placed in the basket shared with another elder.

ENDING THE SESSION:

Share the basket.

Talk about and confirm next session.

AFTER THE SESSION:

Write up comments.

IDEAS FOR MODIFYING THE ACTIVITY: Various techniques may be tried to improve the elder's writing ability. Suggestions for the leader's consideration have been offered by Lunt (1982) and Hale (1981). For example, wrapping the pen or pencil with tape or twisting rubber bands around it may improve writing grasp. The elder may find felt-tip pens easier to use than ball-point pens, and soft lead may be preferred to hard lead in pencils. Larger than normal size pens and pencils are also available and may prove helpful. Clipboards may be used to help hold the paper. A light sprinkle of talcum powder across the paper may help to reduce writing friction.

Various types of magnifying aids are also available. However, these aids should not be recommended without medical consultation.

If the machines are available, typing or tape-recording the poetry might be a suitable alternative to writing.

TIPS FOR SAFETY: Make sure lighting is adequate. Choose a work area that allows the elder to sit and write comfortably. Watch for signs of frustration, confusion, and/or fatigue.

Do not rush this activity; allow for periods of rest as desired.

UNIT NAME: Literature

ACTIVITY PLAN 4: POETRY TO MUSIC

PURPOSE OF ACTIVITY: To encourage interest in writing poetry through the use of music.

DESCRIPTION OF ACTIVITY: The leader and elder will listen to a variety of musical selections and then express, through talking and writing, the feelings the music inspires.

BENEFITS OF ACTIVITY: Music can have an inspiring effect and help to make writing poetry an enjoyable experience. It also helps one to identify and express various emotions. In addition, this activity, stimulates creative thinking, promotes sensory awareness, and encourages talking together.

BEFORE THE SESSION:

   Things to do

The leader should collect a variety of records or cassette tapes that can be played during the session. These can be musical records/tapes as well as records/tapes of sounds such as the ocean or bird calls. The public library and the Library of Congress are excellent sources for these records or tapes. The leader should review the music to get an idea of the variety of sensations, moods, feelings, and memories the music can inspire.

Things to take

Musical selections (on records or tapes)
Phonograph or tape player
Paper, pen, or pencil

WHAT TO DO DURING THE SESSION:

Greeting and opening chat; pay attention to any immediate needs.

Complete any unfinished business from previous session.

Explain the session's activities.

The leader briefly describes the session and chats with the elder about the kind of music he/she enjoys.

Do activities.

First, the leader and elder listen to a couple of selections and share their thoughts on what the music makes them see, feel, think, and/or remember.

After this introduction, listen to a new record or tape and encourage the elder to write down the feelings or thoughts inspired by the music. No particular writing format is required. Try listening for a while, writing down a word or line, and listening again. It is best to use records without singing since words can be distracting.

A sentence "starter" such as "The music reminds me. . ." or "The music makes me feel . . ." may help the elder begin writing.

The leader is encouraged to write poetry to the music, also! After poems are created, read them aloud to one another. Be sure to save the poems. These poems can be shared with others, saved in scrapbooks, or featured in newsletters.

Session wrap-up; enjoy a snack if desired.

The participants can discuss various feelings inspired by the music and how these differed according to the type of music. Plans to save or share the poems can also be discussed. Encourage the elder to create additional poetry, while listening to music, between sessions. Thus, the elder can add to a collection of personal poetry. Reading and sharing the poetry could be a part of future sessions. The leader could also discuss the availability of records or tapes as well as phonographs and/or cassette players if needed. The leader will help the elder contact resources as desired. Resource information is listed in this unit's references.

ENDING THE SESSION:

Share the basket.

Talk about and confirm next session.

AFTER THE SESSION:

Write up comments.

IDEAS FOR MODIFYING THE ACTIVITY: Various techniques may be tried to improve the elder's writing ability. Suggestions for the leader's consideration have been offered by Lunt (1982) and Hale (1981). For example, wrapping the pen or pencil with tape or twisting rubber bands around it may improve writing grasp. The elder may find felt-tip pens easier to use than ball-point pens, and soft lead may be preferred to hard lead in pencils. Larger than normal size pens and pencils are also available and may prove helpful. Clipboards may be used to help hold the paper. A light sprinkle of talcum powder across the paper may help to reduce writing friction.

Various types of magnifying aids are also available. However, these aids should not be recommended without medical consultation.

If the machines are available, typing or tape recording might be a suitable alternative to writing.

The leader may also record responses for the elder; this should be a mutually determined decision.

If listening to music is not possible due to hearing impairment, the leader may try the same activity but substitute a variety of pictures for the music. These pictures may come from magazines and should portray a variety of scenes, events, and situations.

TIPS FOR SAFETY: Conduct the session in a well-lighted area. Choose a work space that allows the elder to sit and write comfortably.

Do not rush the activity; watch for signs of frustration, confusion, and/or fatigue. Allow for periods of rest as desired.

UNIT NAME: Literature

ACTIVITY PLAN 5: WORD PYRAMIDS*

PURPOSE OF ACTIVITY: To involve the elder in a fun and mentally challenging activity.

DESCRIPTION OF ACTIVITY: The leader and elder will fill in the spaces across the pyramid design with letters forming words that fit the number of boxes.

BENEFITS OF ACTIVITY: This activity is both fun and mentally challenging. It stimulates creative thinking, sharpens spelling and vocabulary skills, and also promotes hand-eye coordination.

BEFORE THE SESSION:

   Things to do

The leader prepares the design by starting at the bottom of the pyramid and drawing a long rectangle, dividing it into nine boxes, as shown.

*Adapted from Book of 1000 Family Games, p. 96. Copyright © 1971 The Reader's Digest Association, Inc. Used by permission.

On top of this row, draw a rectangle divided into eight boxes. Continue
to add rows, until the top of the pyramid contains only two boxes,
as shown.

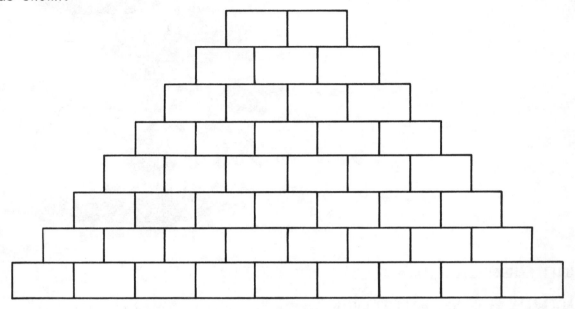

The leader could draw two pyramid designs--one for himself/herself
and one for the elder. Or, the leader may choose to demonstrate how
to draw the pyramid at the beginning of the session and allow the
elder to construct his/her own.

Things to take

Prepared pyramid designs (may be drawn during visit)
Pencils, paper
Dictionary (optional)
Examples of completed pyramids

WHAT TO DO DURING THE SESSION:

Greeting and opening chat; pay attention to any immediate needs.

Complete any unfinished business from previous session.

Explain the session's activities.

Do activities.

Although it is not necessary to choose a topic, this is recommended
as a way to generate interest in the activity. Decide on any topic
of mutual interest: a season, a holiday, a recreational activity,
a location, a famous person, a Bible story, a current event, etc.
Both participants then think of words that relate to the chosen topic
and write them on their individual pyramids. A two-letter word goes
in the top row, a three-letter word in the second row, a four-letter

word in the third row, and so on. Even though the leader and elder are working separately on their pyramids, they may help each other.

To emphasize vocabulary building, players should give the meaning of unfamiliar words. Although the use of a dictionary is probably not needed, it remains optional. More difficult topics may be chosen as the visit progresses.

Session wrap-up; enjoy a snack if desired.

ENDING THE SESSION:

Share the basket.

Talk about and confirm next session.

AFTER THE SESSION:

Write up comments.

IDEAS FOR MODIFYING THE ACTIVITY: Various techniques may be tried to improve the elder's writing ability. Suggestions for the leader's consideration have been offered by Lunt (1982) and Hale (1981). For example, wrapping the pen or pencil with tape or twisting rubber bands around it may improve writing grasp. The elder may find felt-tip pens easier to use than ball-point pens, and soft lead may be preferred to hard lead in pencils. Larger than normal size pens and pencils are also available and may prove helpful. Clipboards may be used to help hold the paper. A light sprinkle of talcum powder across the paper may help to reduce writing friction.

It is possible to participate in this activity without using the pyramid design. If this proves to be too much of a problem, then write the numbers 2 to 9 on a piece of paper. Next to the 2, write a two-letter word, next to the 3, write a three-letter word, and so on.

TIPS FOR SAFETY: Lighting should be adequate and fall properly so that the work area is well covered. Conduct the activity in a work area that allows the elder to sit and write comfortably.

UNIT NAME: Literature

ACTIVITY PLAN 6: READING ALOUD

PURPOSE OF ACTIVITY: To involve the elder in a pleasurable activity that may revive or create interest in reading.

DESCRIPTION OF ACTIVITY: The leader or elder will read aloud from a favorite book, play, magazine article, or other material while the other listens.

BENEFITS OF ACTIVITY: The most important value of reading aloud is pleasure. In addition, reading aloud helps develop new interests, provides information, and promotes interaction. Reading aloud involves speaking, listening, and concentration skills. It may also help one to understand and express his/her emotions.

BEFORE THE SESSION:

   Things to do

The leader should select some reading materials from which he/she can read aloud to the elder. The leader might select a favorite book, play, biographical sketch, inspirational reading, Bible reading, or poem. The readings can be short or long, real or fictional, about holidays, people, nature, science, or any other subject.

The leader should allow the elder to help with the selection of the reading material. The elder may have some favorite books from which he/she would like the leader to read. The local public library is an excellent source for selecting reading materials and receiving other assistance.

Things to take

Reading materials of various types (as described above)

WHAT TO DO DURING THE SESSION:

Greeting and opening chat; pay attention to any immediate needs.

Complete any unfinished business from previous session.

Explain the session's activities.

The leader briefly describes the session and may ask for the elder's assistance in selecting a story to read aloud.

Do activities.

The leader or elder begins to read from the selected material. The reader should pause occasionally for questions, comments, or reactions. At the conclusion both will discuss the reading as desired.

Session wrap-up; enjoy a snack if desired.

The leader and elder should discuss interest in pursuing reading activities. The leader will provide information about the availability of books with large print, books and magazines available on cassette tapes or records, cassette players available for checkout from the public library, and other possible resources. The leader will help the elder contact these resources as desired. Resource information is listed in this unit's references.

ENDING THE SESSION:

Share the basket.

Talk about and confirm next session.

AFTER THE SESSION:

Write up comments.

IDEAS FOR MODIFYING THE ACTIVITY: Check with local bookstores and public libraries concerning the availability of large-print editions of books and magazines. If the participant cannot read large print or is unable to hold a book and turn pages, he/she is probably eligible for Talking Books (Lunt, 1982). Consult references at the end of this unit.

Various book holders, both commercially manufactured and homemade, are available. These include holders designed for lapboards, tables, and bed trays as well as free-standing and/or suspended book holders.

Various types of magnifying aids are also available. However, these aids should not be recommended without medical consultation.

"To help turn pages, use the eraser of a pencil, buy a rubber finger cover, or dip a finger into Tacky Fingers (available at stationery stores)" (Lunt, 1982, p. 114). "Sometimes when the fingers cannot be used but there is good control of the arm, pages can be turned with the side of the hand or the elbow if a book or magazine is lying flat" (Hale, 1981, p. 30).

TIPS FOR SAFETY: Make sure the lighting is adequate and falls properly so that enough light is shed on the book (Hale, 1982).

No specific precautions are necessary other than sensitivity to the general well-being of the participant. Watch for signs of tiring.

UNIT NAME: Literature

ACTIVITY PLAN 7: SPOKEN SCRAPBOOK

PURPOSE OF ACTIVITY: To allow the elder and leader to learn more about each other.

DESCRIPTION OF ACTIVITY: The leader and the elder will collect and share information describing favorite hobbies, family history, favorite memories, and the like.

BENEFITS OF ACTIVITY: It's fun to talk about oneself! Sharing bits of information about each other also stimulates self-awareness and self-expression, encourages talking and interacting together, and helps discover similar interests and experiences.

BEFORE THE SESSION:

    Things to do

    Things to take

Items the leader wishes to share when discussing his/her own interests.

WHAT TO DO DURING THE SESSION:

    Greeting and opening chat; pay attention to any immediate needs.

Complete any unfinshed business from previous session.

Explain this session's activities.

Explain that the elder will have an opportunity to discuss something about himself/herself. Possible topics could include "my favorite hobbies," "wishes I have," "things that make me happy," "about my family," "things I have accomplished during my lifetime," "my work experiences," "places I have visited," etc.

Do activities.

After hearing the explanation of the session, the elder begins to think of something that describes certain things about himself/herself. A photo album, family Bible, or postards might help to get the discussion going.

Session wrap-up; enjoy a snack if desired.

Explain to the elder that these topics could be used when writing poetry.

ENDING THE SESSION:

Share the basket.

Talk about and confirm next session.

AFTER THE SESSION:

Write up comments.

IDEAS FOR MODIFYING THE ACTIVITY: The leader could bring an empty photo album and fill the pages with pictures, newspaper clippings, invitations, and other items the elder shares during the session. The photo album may be an additional expense for the leader. The elder should be encouraged to pay for such an item. If cost is a factor, the leader may choose to bring a pouch file folder to store the collection of items.

TIPS FOR SAFETY: Be sensitive to how the elder is feeling; watch for signs of fatigue.

REFERENCES AND RESOURCES

American Foundation for the Blind.* 15 West 16th Street, New York, NY 10011. Offers aids and appliances, information on how a blind person gets around, how to integrate aging persons who are visually handicapped into community senior programs, recreation and the blind adult, directory of agencies serving the visually handicapped in the United States, and products for people with vision problems.

Choice Magazine Listening.* 14 Maple Street, Port Washington, NY 10050. Offers subscriptions to a series of records, each of which includes selections of articles, fiction, and poetry culled from various popular magazines, to be used with Talking Books record players.

Cornett, C. E., & Charles, F. Bibliotherapy: The right book at the right time. Bloomington, IN: Phi Delta Kappa Educational Foundation, 1980.

Division for the Blind and Physically Handicapped.* Library of Congress, Washington, DC 20542. Provides applications for the Talking Books Program and refers applicant to the nearest cooperating library or agency. Collection of braille and recorded materials for eligible readers.

Going, M. E. Hospital libraries and work with the disabled. London: The Library Association, 1973.

Hale, G. (Ed.). The source book for the disabled. New York: Bantam Books, 1981.

Hamill, C. M., & Oliver, R. C. Therapeutic activities for the handicapped elderly, Appendix E. Rockville, MD: Aspen Systems Corporation, 1980.

Insight. Madison, WI: Bi-Folkal Productions, Fall 1983.

Koch, K. Wishes, lies, and dreams: Teaching children to write poetry. New York: Harper & Row, 1970.

Koch, K. I never told anybody: Teaching poetry writing in a nursing home. New York: Random House, 1977.

Lunt, S. A handbook for the disabled: Ideas and inventions for easier living. New York: Charles Scribner, 1982.

McNiff, S. The arts and psychotherapy. Springfield, IL: Charles C. Thomas, 1981.

Peterson, C. S., & Hall, B. Story programs: A source book of materials. Metuchen, NJ: Scarecrow Press, 1980.

Phinney, E. (Ed.). <u>The librarian and the patient</u>. Chicago: American Library Association, 1977.

Recording for the Blind, Inc.* 215 East 58th Street, New York, NY 10022. Publishes <u>The News of the Week Review</u>, as well as tapes, textbooks for college students, and foreign language recordings.

Adapted Activity Equipment*

<u>Magnifying Reader with Stand</u>
For reading or fine craft work; adjusts up and down. The magnifier can be detached for hand use.
Supplier: Fred Sammons, Inc.

<u>Type with One Hand Booklet</u>
For the one-handed typist
Supplier: Fred Sammons, Inc.

<u>Right-Line Paper</u>
Narrow and wide rule, 250 sheets each. For those who have difficulty in following the lines of regular paper; made with raised lines superimposed on the printed lines.
Supplier: Modern Education Corporation

<u>Marks Script Guide</u>
Allows writing within a 3/4-inch space. A guide moves up and down one line at a time and a margin stop can be moved to the left or right.
Supplier: American Foundation for the Blind.

Suppliers*

American Foundation for the Blind
Consumer Products Division
15 West 16th Street
New York, NY 10011

Modern Education Corporation
P.O. Box 721
Tulsa, OK 74101

Fred Sammons, Inc.
Box 32
Brookfield, IL 60513

*These and other suggestions for adapted activity equipment are found in Hamill, C. M., & Oliver, R. C. <u>Therapeutic activities for the handicapped elderly</u> (Appendix B, pp. 261-265; Appendix E, pp. 275-278). Rockville, MD: Aspen Systems Corporation, 1980. Reprinted with permission of Aspen Publishers, Inc.

CHAPTER 10

Remembering the Past Activity Plans

UNIT NAME: Remembering the Past

ACTIVITY PLAN 2: ORAL HISTORY INTRODUCTION (The first activity in all recreation units should be "Assessing Recreation Interests." See pages 55 to 57.)

PURPOSE OF ACTIVITY: To explain how oral history has served immigrants to the United States, pioneers settling areas of the country, and families regaining a record of their roots.

DESCRIPTION OF ACTIVITY: An oral history from a senior will be read. Areas of interest in the elder's life will be identified for future sessions and a method for collecting and transcribing these bits of history will be discussed.

BENEFITS OF ACTIVITY: The elder will be introduced to oral history indirectly without needing to reveal personal history. Talking about the past is a natural activity and fits easily into a one-to-one situation.

BEFORE THE SESSION:

Things to

Things to take

WHAT TO DO DURING THE SESSION:

Greeting and opening chat; pay attention to any immediate needs.

Complete any unfinished business from previous session.

Explain the session's activities.

This unit can include a detailed way to record oral history information from the elder. A tape recorder may be used in many sessions. The leader can take tapes home and during the week write or type some historical facts discussed in the previous session. The tape and written record may then be returned to the elder during the next session. The tapes should be left with the elder once they are full. No other use of the recorded history will be made.

Do activities.

Oral histories have been used as a means of better understanding the past as seen through the life experiences of older people who lived and worked while this history was being made. In a Washington, DC listening project for senior citizens, 100 people told their stories of what happened during all those years. They ranged in age from early sixties to late nineties. Here is one person's life review from that St. Alban's Church Project. The leader or elder reads Lawrence Jackson's history (Jenkins, 1978, pp. 21-26).*

I was born in Orange County, Virginia, in a small rural community of colored people. We call ourselves black now, but in those days we were colored. The community was named Jacksontown. It was named Jacksontown because all the people, with the exception of one family, had the name Jackson. They were not necessarily related, but this was a carryover after the time of freedom from slavery; people just took names. I really don't know what prompted all these people to take the name Jackson, but that is what they took.

My own family name really should not have been Jackson. I dug back in history and found a little story behind that which I suppose I should tell. My paternal grandfather's mother was a Cherokee Indian and his father was white. After the Civil War, she married a black man. My grandfather, who was in his late adolescence or early twenties at that time, carried the name of his real father. But his stepfather told him, "Now, son, you need to take my name because it is not respectful for a colored man to have a white man's name." When the story was told, we laughed about it because of course all black people took the names of whites. But that is how my grandfather happened to be a Jackson rather than the name which he inherited in his early youth.

This community was rather close-knit and mostly farmers. My father was the one carpenter; in fact he was the only one who was not a farmer. We had a very small plot of land. His father, my grandfather, had been a carpenter before him; and my grandfather had been sent by his father to Williamsport, Pennsylvania, to be an apprentice carpenter. This was before the Civil War and of course my grandfather never really was a slave, because his mother, being an Indian, was free.

---

*From S. Jenkins, <u>Past, present: Recording life histories of older people</u>. Washington, DC: St. Alban's Parish, 1978. Used by permission.

Anyway, we lived in this small community, and when most of the people there built their new houses they tore down their old cabins that they lived in. My grandmother had insisted that she wanted to keep her cabin so our new house was built against the old cabin. The cabin really became our family room. It was the kitchen, it was where we played, where we studied, where we sat. It had a fireplace. In later years they had put in one of the old-time ranges. That was where we cooked. It had a warmer over the top where the leftovers from breakfast were placed, and we would go back and swipe a biscuit.

I was the baby in the family for a long time, and I just loved biscuits. I would go to the warmer and get a biscuit until my grandmother said to me, "Boy, leave those biscuits alone. If you eat anymore you are going to burst wide open and a piece will fly out here and another piece will fly out there and then your mama won't have any more baby." It frightened me to death. I left the biscuits alone for quite a long while.

My first job was thinning corn. We had a little stick that we had made especially for this and we went into the fields about 4 hours in the morning to thin corn. I don't know how old I was then, but I was very young. At noon we were paid by the owner of the farm. We were paid in dimes, 10¢ an hour. Of course that was a tremendous amount of money in those days. One of the farmhands tried to trade his nickels for our dimes because he said that the nickels were larger and therefore they were worth more. Well, we knew better. Our parents had taught us the value of money. We politely declined his offer and went on our way.

I also went into berry fields with my grandmother picking blackberries. We called them "dewberries" or "lowberries." They grew on the ground. They were big luscious things. When you got through, your hands were all scarred and scratched, but we enjoyed it.

What we enjoyed most of all was seeing our grandmother carry the load of berries back home. She carried one bucket in each hand and one on her head. She balanced this 2-gallon bucket of berries on her head as easily as we carried one in our hand, and the fact is that she would actually climb over the rail fence with this basket of berries on her head. We just did not see how she did this. She had very beautiful carriage. She, too, was a mixture of Indian and Negro. I suppose this business of carrying things on her head was a throwback to her African ancestors. She was a very dignified woman.

We went to church at the Baptist Church in the community. People, of course, shouted. Grandma never joined in the shouting. But it was obvious that she was emotionally affected by the songs and so forth. And lo and behold, on one Sunday we turned around and looked and Grandma was up shouting. We just thought that was the most wonderful thing. But we never saw it happen again because she was conscious of the fact that we were a little bit amused. She never shouted again. That is, I never saw her shout.

My first job was at $45 a month teaching elementary school. By that time my mother had died and my father had broken up housekeeping. I went to live with my aunt and uncle. My aunt was a community worker, and she said that I should devote my life to serving my people. She

persuaded me to take this job at $45 a month and I took it. I paid
$17.50 for room and board. I slept in the bed with another fellow,
who was the principal of this small school.

(A continuation of Mr. Jackson's story will be part of next session,
School Days.)

   Session wrap-up; enjoy a snack if desired.

The elder and leader can discuss similarities and differences in the
recollections of Mr. Jackson and their own growing years.

ENDING THE SESSION:

   Share the basket.

   Talk about and confirm next session.

For the next session the leader may bring a small tape recorder and
record the conversations. This information may be partly written
out by the leader during the subsequent week. At the end of the unit,
the elder and leader will make a book of this written oral record.

AFTER THE SESSION:

   Write up comments.

Jotting down notes about the elder's past as discussed in this session
may prove rewarding.

IDEAS FOR MODIFYING THE ACTIVITY: The leader and elder may share
the oral reading, or the leader may need to read all of the text.

TIPS FOR SAFETY: Good light for reading will be important.

UNIT NAME: Remembering the Past

ACTIVITY PLAN 3: SCHOOL DAYS

PURPOSE OF ACTIVITY: To recall and record highlights of the school experiences of the elder and leader.

DESCRIPTION OF ACTIVITY: The elder and leader will finish reading the history of Mr. Jackson and recall their own past school experiences.

BENEFITS OF ACTIVITY: Information is shared in a natural conversational mode. School experiences are something everyone has experienced at some time. This topic then provides a universal starting point for telling personal stories. Persons with short-term memory problems will still be able to relate memories from their youth.

BEFORE THE SESSION:

   Things to do

Collect any pictures or materials that relate to the leader's school days. Old yearbooks are perfect.

   Things to take

School pictures and other memorabilia

WHAT TO DO DURING THE SESSION:

   Greeting and opening chat; pay attention to any immediate needs.

Complete any unfinished business from previous session.

Explain the session's activities.

Do activities.

1. Read another section of Lawrence Jackson's history, from the St. Alban's Church Project in Washington, DC (Jenkins, 1978, pp. 27-32).

I must tell this: I believe firmly in school discipline. I have mixed emotions about corporal punishment, but I got my share of it and it didn't harm me. When we were chastised at school and we got home, the word was there in advance, and Mama and Grandma would say, "Put your books down and go get your switch." There was an orchard out the back, and we got a switch and brought it in to get our whipping for getting whipped at school. If it wasn't the right kind of switch, we were sent back again.

So in this school where I taught I had a boy in my classroom who was quite a bully. He bullied the other children and he tested me. I had resolved that I would not do any whipping in school even though we were permitted to do so. My predecessor had left a very ample strap which he had used. This particular day the boy had cut up terribly, had tried me, and had tried the other youngsters. Finally he slapped a girl very severely.

I said, "Well, this is it."

So I called him up to my desk and he refused to come. I knew that this was a test and I insisted, but he said, "No, I am not coming."

I said, "Well then, I will have to come after you."

I went down for him, and he humped up as if to protect himself against me. He drew his little fist back; he was going to hit me. I thought to myself, "I will have to do this." So I grabbed him and gave him a good one across the seat.

He sat down and he fussed all the afternoon. He was going to get his older brothers and his cousins and this one and that one to beat me up, to slice me up. I knew that his cousins and brothers were bad rascals because I had heard about them. So I said, "Come what may," and I sat down at the close of school and wrote his grandmother a letter. I knew he lived with his grandmother. The post office was right down the street, and I knew that she would get the letter so I dropped it there.

The next morning as we sat at the breakfast table we looked out of the window and here was this old lady coming with a big walking stick, and the principal said, "Here she comes." And he had business elsewhere.

So she came and she knocked. Bam, bam, bam! I went to the door.

She said, "You Mister Jackson?"

I said, "Yes, ma'am," in a nervous voice.

She said, "I got your letter. You told me you beat that boy."

I said, "Yes, ma'am."

She said, "I come to tell you that I have beat him too." And the world of burden rolled away at that point. I knew that she was with me, and I had no more trouble out of that youngster.

2. Discuss the elder's first day in school or his/her very first memory of school days.

3. Allow the elder to do as much talking as possible, with the leader trying to detail his/her own recollections in response to comments by the elder or when the elder can no longer recall events.

4. Discuss schools today.

    Session wrap-up; enjoy a snack if desired.

ENDING THE SESSION:

    Share the basket.

    Talk about and confirm next session.

Next session will center on health problems in the past. Assure the elder that personal information need not be shared if that is too private. The two will discuss other general topics, such as home remedies and how medicine was practiced in the past.

AFTER THE SESSION:

    Write up comments.

IDEAS FOR MODIFYING THE SESSION: The leader may bring a child to the session to share in stories about school today. If this is done, it should be cleared with the elder during the previous session. A child younger than 8 years may be too young to stay attentive for an hour.

TIPS FOR SAFETY:

UNIT NAME: Remembering the Past

ACTIVITY PLAN 4: HEALTH PROBLEMS

PURPOSE OF ACTIVITY: To reflect on medical treatments of the past and the health history of the elder's and leader's family.

DESCRIPTION OF ACTIVITY: The leader will read the piece about the importance of one person's health history in tracing a disease that struck a grandchild. Both will then re-create their own family medical history.

BENEFITS OF ACTIVITY: The elder can better understand the importance of keeping personal historical information. The leader and elder will create a written record of health facts for their own families. The final product from this unit, a recorded written history of the elder, will begin to materialize as the results of the last three sessions are compiled.

BEFORE THE SESSION:

   Things to do

If the previous school days session did not allow time for both to share school days stories, then the leader may want to prepare his/her own medical history before this session. This will allow more time to center on the elder's history.

   Things to take

WHAT TO DO DURING THE SESSION:

Greeting and opening chat; pay attention to any immediate needs.

Complete any unfinished business from previous session.

If the leader has been keeping a written record of the elder's history, he/she can read the transcribed highlights of the previous sessions and ask if the elder feels this summary is a good record of what was shared.

Explain the session's activities.

Do activities.

1. Read from Leone Noble Western's <u>The Gold Key to Writing Your Life History</u> (Western, 1980, pp. 26-27).*

   One day a mature student of mine phoned, and uttered an unexpected word of thanks for something I had done. "Thank you, for saving my grandson's life," she said. I did not even know the grandson, but the story did involve me--more specifically, the course (writing your own life history)--in a roundabout way. The woman's 17-year-old grandson, an outstanding high school athlete, had been stricken with a serious blood disease just 2 months prior to the phone call. The illness was baffling, and medical specialists whom the family consulted were unable to diagnose it or treat it. The young man suffered greatly, and his health deteriorated at an alarming rate for several weeks.
   One evening just before Christmas, when the youth's parents stopped at the grandmother's on their way home from visiting him, the ailing youth's father made the observation that "If only we knew more about our family's health history, maybe we could help the doctors when they keep asking if anybody else in the family has ever had anything similar to Jay's condition."
   The grandmother jumped up and rushed across the room. She brought her card file box back to the table where they were drinking coffee. Opening the box, she said, "I didn't tell you, but I'm going to a college class to learn to write my life history. I wanted to surprise you."
   Well, it was a spendid surprise, for she produced her own father's health card. He had died at the age of 45, when the grandmother was but 12 years old, from what was apparently the same disease as her young grandson's! Immediately, the father called the doctor, read him details from the file card, and told even more that his mother-in-law had remembered--anything which might be helpful in curing Jay. The doctor was able to begin treating the disease with modern drugs not even considered before, which literally saved the life of her grandson. Within a few short months he was back in school "rarin' to go," as she said.

*From L. N. Western, <u>The gold key to writing your life history</u>. Port Angeles, WA: Peninsula Publishing, 1980. Used by permission.

2. Read the spoken health history of Vince Waters, born 1913 (Jenkins, 1978, p. 38):

As a child I had the pneumonia pretty bad. We called it double pneumonia. My mother heated salt in bags and put it on each one of my thighs. If you caught a cold, they would cook the lamb and then take the mutton tallow and grease your chest with that. My aunt was telling me that her mother would take pot liquor and let it get cold and grease her grandson's legs. He had the rickets, and that's what she used to do. I remember my grandfather coming to my house one time when I had a bad sore throat, and he took a quill and blew sulphur down my throat, and it really got better. We used a lot of different things like that that were unusual and they really did help.

3. Discuss health practices in the elder's life. For flavor, include old-time remedies. The elder may have been raised on a farm or homestead. If so, he/she probably remembers the preparations for the long, hard winters, which may have included killing skunks and geese so that grease could be rendered from them. The grease was used for treatment of colds and lung congestions.

Session wrap-up; enjoy a snack if desired.

ENDING THE SESSION:

Share the basket.

Talk about and confirm next session.

During the next session, the elder and leader will center their remembrances around travel experiences. The elder may wish to look for pictures or souvenirs from past trips in preparation for the session.

AFTER THE SESSION:

Write up comments.

IDEAS FOR MODIFYING THE ACTIVITY:

TIPS FOR SAFETY:

UNIT NAME: Remembering the Past

ACTIVITY PLAN 5: TRAVEL

PURPOSE OF ACTIVITY: To remember and record the moving and vacation experiences of the elder and leader.

DESCRIPTION OF ACTIVITY: The elder and leader will discuss their travel experiences. Both will also view photographs from trips and travel magazines.

BENEFITS OF ACTIVITY: Travel experiences are usually positive memories, with colorful images of places, foods, and people. The elder and leader may find places they both have visited. Recalling such travels allows the elder to move mentally out of his/her home environment.

BEFORE THE SESSION:

Things to do

1. Collect photos and souvenirs from the leader's own travels and record a written record of the most memorable trips in his/her past.

2. Locate magazines with pictures of the places the elder mentioned at the close of the last session. Libraries have travel books and National Geographic magazines. The American Automobile Association or other travel agency can also serve as a resource for the leader.

Things to take

Photos and magazines

WHAT TO DO DURING THE SESSION:

Greeting and opening chat; pay attention to any immediate needs.

Complete any unfinished business from previous session.

Explain the session's activities.

Do activities.

1. Read the following story about a travel experience from the author of this oral history unit.

   We took a trip by train from Merida, Yucatan, Mexico, to Planque, a Mayan Indian ruin. We were traveling at night on a sleeper car. The conductor called out in the morning, "Planque," and we all jumped up and dressed quickly, expecting the next stop to be ours. The sleeper car was the last car on the train, and so it had bounced around quite a bit during the night. When the train stopped, we were so far back on the train that we couldn't see the station's name. Knowing that the train would start again soon, I became nervous and jumped off the train. My family didn't follow me immediately, and as I walked closer to the station, I began to make out the letters on the depot. At the same time the train started moving forward. In one second's time I realized three things: The name on the depot was not long enough to spell Planque, my family was five cars back yelling and waving at me, and the train was picking up speed. In what little Spanish I knew I asked a Mexican gentleman on the train, "Es Planque?" He responded, "No," and reached an arm out for me. While running next to the train, I threw my bag and then one leg aboard. With some tugging and pulling by others I was once more safely on the train, though visibly shaken. When my knees stopped shaking, I walked back to the sleeper car. Along the way I passed the conductor, who shook a scolding finger at me while wearing a big grin. My family made such fun of my impatience, and to this day they remind me of that adventure whenever I start to do something too soon, without a little forethought.

2. Begin recording stories and experiences from the elder's history. Refer to any pictures that may apply.

   Session wrap-up; enjoy a snack if desired.

ENDING THE SESSION:

Share the basket.

Talk about and confirm next session.

AFTER THE SESSION:

Write up comments.

IDEAS FOR MODIFYING THE ACTIVITY:

TIPS FOR SAFETY:

UNIT NAME: Remembering the Past

ACTIVITY PLAN 6: JOBS

PURPOSE OF ACTIVITY: To identify and record the work history of the United States through the recollections of an immigrant and of the elder and leader.

DESCRIPTION OF ACTIVITY: This session centers on the work history as read from <u>American Mosaic: The Immigrant Experience in the Words of Those Who Lived It</u> and as discussed by the elder and leader.

BENEFITS OF ACTIVITY: This session has value as a means of recording an important aspect of American culture as seen through the eyes of workers or their families.

BEFORE THE SESSION:

    Things to do

    Things to take

WHAT TO DO DURING THE SESSION:

    Greeting and opening chat; pay attention to any immediate needs.

    Complete any unfinshed business from previous session.

    Explain the session's activities.

Do activities.

1. Read Vera Gurchikov's recollection's of her family's work in the mines after they immigrated to the United States from Austria-Hungary in 1911.[*]

   We married and he worked in the mine all his life. He worked 10 hours a day, 6 days a week, and no money. He worked in the mine and we lived in a company house. It was right here, up the road about a mile. The mine gave a house, a company house. It cost $6.00 a month. But my husband made only $1.50 a day. There was a company store--only a company store, no other stores. We bought all our food and everything from the company store. Payday came, everything came out of the pay. They kept us right down, you know. We couldn't move, couldn't go anywhere. Only a little train to go to Wharton, to do a little shopping. We had it rough here. The bosses had a hand on us in the mine, in the company house, all the time. There was no place to go, just stay here.
   There was a man here, a Russian; he worked for the mine, like a boss, a supervisor in the mine. He had a good job. The mine wanted men, he telled everybody. They wrote letters to the other side, and they sent more men; because the mine was killing men. Work in the mine was dangerous, very dangerous. The bosses knew it, but there was no other way in them days. It was the only way they could get work done. That's why they got young boys from the other side. They keeped pushing them in the mine, pushing them in. A lot of young men, young boys, came over, and they be killed off in the mine, just like that. They had a cemetery, right next to the mine. They keeped sending back to the other side for more boys. (Morrison, 1980, p. 59)

2. Begin discussing memories of jobs and work experiences in the elder's and leader's past.

   Session wrap-up; enjoy a snack if desired.

ENDING THE SESSION:

   Share the basket.

   Talk about and confirm next session.

During the next session a book will be made for this unit. A cloth covering can be used to make this book. If the elder has any material that he/she would like to use in covering the book, it can be located during the week. Three pieces, about 12 in. x 18 in., will be needed.

[*]From J. Morrison and C. F. Zabusky, <u>American mosaic: The immigrant experience in the words of those who lived it</u>. New York: E. P. Dutton, 1980. ©E. P. Dutton 1980. Used by permission.

AFTER THE SESSION:

   Write up comments.

IDEAS FOR MODIFYING THE ACTIVITY:

TIPS FOR SAFETY:

UNIT NAME: Remembering the Past

ACTIVITY PLAN 7: CREATING A BOOK

PURPOSE OF ACTIVITY: To consolidate the activities of this unit. To make a book that summarizes the elder's history, which can be given to family members as a gift.

DESCRIPTION OF ACTIVITY: The leader and elder will make cloth covers for the written text or collected materials reflecting the elder's history. The photos that were collected to accompany the history and the cassette tapes of the recorded sessions (if taken) will be included in pouches inside this book.

BENEFITS OF ACTIVITY: The elder will feel a sense of accomplishment as the final product of the unit is completed. There is the possibility of enjoying creative ideas in making and decorating the book. The book is about the elder and gives a sense of "I am important!" The final product will make a very meaningful gift for someone special.

BEFORE THE SESSION:

Things to do

1. The leader may wish to make a book cover in advance of this session to use as a model for the elder and to allow more time to help the elder.

2. Locate three squares of material, 12 in. x 18 in.

3. Locate two pieces of cloth ribbon, 6 in. to 8 in.

4. Type or write the highlights from the elder's recollections from previous sessions.

    Things to take

Cloth pieces
Ribbons
Stapler with staples or fasteners
Written texts of elder's oral history
Charts for family trees
One package of iron-on seam binding
Scissors, thread, needle, and thimble
Iron
All session cassette tapes and written records

WHAT TO DO DURING THE SESSION:

Greeting and opening chat; pay attention to any immediate needs.

Complete any unfinished business from previous session.

Explain the session's activities.

Do activities.

The following illustrations will help when reading the directions:

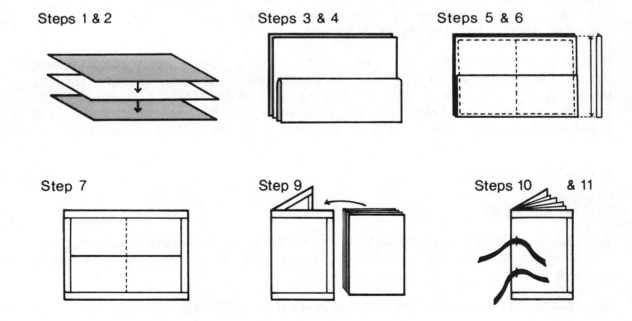

Steps 1 & 2   Steps 3 & 4   Steps 5 & 6

Step 7   Step 9   Steps 10   & 11

Steps 12 & 13   Step 14

Step 15   Step 16

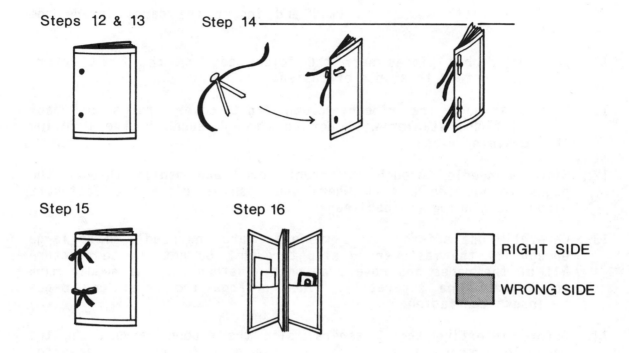

RIGHT SIDE

WRONG SIDE

1. Cut out the three pieces of material, 12 in. x 18 in., for each book, if not done in advance.

2. Lay the pieces directly on top of one another with the following sides up: piece one, wrong side up; piece two, right side up; piece three, wrong side up.

3. Fold down the top edge of piece three until the top edge is even with the bottom edges of pieces one and two (fold it in half lengthwise).

4. Press these three pieces, making the folded piece smooth and flat. This folded piece will be a pouch on the inside of the front and back covers.

5. Using a sewing machine or stitching by hand, baste the pieces together 1/4 inch in from the cut edges, and crosswise in the middle.

6. Cut lengths of iron-on seam binding to be exactly the length of each of the sides of the square.

7. Iron on the seam binding while folding it in half over the raw cut edges of the cloth squares. This finishes off the edges of the cover and gives a nice colored border.

8. Arrange the history pages with the family tree as page one and the others as desired.

9. Fold the cloth square in half and insert the pages inside the fold.

10. Lay two ribbon pieces near the folded edge on the front cover, where you intend to staple or fasten.

11. Staple through the ribbon, cloth front cover, pages and back cover (if the stapler will not go through such thickness follow the remaining plan).

12. Stick a needle through the front cover and gently through the pages to provide a mark where you wish to place the fasteners along the binding (folded) edge.

13. Carefully use scissors or a knife to make the needle marks large enough for the fastener to slip through. Do not try to puncture all of the pages and covers at once; instead use the needle mark to do each one separately. Then arrange the cover and pages to insert the fasteners.

14. Before inserting the fasteners, slip the ribbon between the two bendable prongs of the fastener. Once a fastener is inserted through all of the materials, spread the prongs on the back side of the book to secure it in place.

15. Whether the staple method or the fastener method is used, the ribbons can now be tied into bows.

16. Place the poems or verses and pictures in the front inside pouch and the cassette tapes in the back inside pouch.

   Session wrap-up; enjoy a snack if desired.

Take time to look at the finished product.

ENDING THE SESSION:

   Share the basket.

   Talk about and confirm next session.

AFTER THE SESSION:

   Write up comments.

IDEAS FOR MODIFYING THE ACTIVITY: The book can be bound in other ways. Businesses that duplicate materials often have machines that bind materials with plastic bindings, and they offer a selection of

colored covers. This would mean the leader must make a special trip
to the business and pay the small fee for such binding; however, if
the elder and leader are not able to follow the directions described
in this activity plan, professional help may be welcome. Also, if
the elder or leader enjoys embroidery, the cloth covers can be stitched
before or after assembling the book. An attractive book can also
be made using a photo album or scrapbook.

TIPS FOR SAFETY: Use of the iron must be supervised by the leader
so as not to chance burning the elder or starting a fire. The leader
should be very careful making holes in the cloth and paper. Trying
to put a hole in material that is too thick can result in the scissors
or knife slipping and puncturing the supporting hand. Resting the
material on a stack of newspapers instead of the palm of the hand,
and attempting to puncture only one layer at a time will make this
step safe. When the session is over, make certain the work area is
cleaned and the iron is turned off, cooled, and stored.

REFERENCES AND RESOURCES

Erickson, L. M., & Leide, K. Bi-folkal productions: Resources for sharing the remembered past. Madison, WI: Bi-folkal Productions, 1985.

Good old days. Tower Press, Seabrook, NH. (Monthly subscriptions available)

Jenkins, S. Past, present: Recording life histories of older people. Washington, DC: St. Alban's Parish, 1978.

Morrison, J. & Zabusky, C. F. American mosaic: The immigrant experience in the words of those who lived it. New York: E. P. Dutton, 1980.

Western, L. N. The gold key to writing your life history. Port Angeles, WA: Peninsula Publishing, 1980.

APPENDICES

APPENDIX A
Audiovisuals

Slides that depict vision changes in the aged:

Vision Kit
Dr. Leon Postalan
The Gerontology Center
University of Michigan
Ann Arbor, MI

(Dr. Postalan's slides are accompanied by a script.)

Vision Kit
Dr. Gary Ross
Gerontology Program
University of Nebraska at Omaha
Omaha, NE

(Dr. Ross's slides have a tape that can be played on a cassette tape recorder to accompany the slides.)

Goggles that change the inclination of the floor and depict visual difficulties encountered in walking may be obtained from

Goggles Kit
Pentagon Services Corporation
21 Harriet Drive
Syosset, NY 11791

Tapes that depict hearing changes as a person gets older:

Hearing Tape
Dr. Gary Ross
Gerontology Program
University of Nebraska at Omaha
Omaha, NE

Getting Through (record)
1970 Zenith Corporation
6501 West Grand Avenue
Chicago, IL 60635

Books

Leonard Biegel's
The Best Years Catalogue
A Source Book for Older Americans
Publisher: G. P. Putnam's Sons, 1978

Films

1. Out of Left Field

16 mm, color, 7 minutes. Features blind and visually impaired youth
participating in recreational activities such as trampoline, rhythms,
cards, baseball, singing, and dancing. Available through the American
Foundation for the Blind, 15 West 16th Street, New York, NY 10011.

2. A Matter of Inconvenience

16 mm, color, 10 minutes. Focuses on skiing and the adaptations
possible for people with various impairments, including amputee and
blind skiers. Available from Standfield House Films/Media, 12381
Wilshire Boulevard, Suite 203, Los Angeles, CA 90025.

3. It's Ability That Counts

16 mm, color, 32 minutes. Features the new and modern sports facility
at the National Spinal Injury Center in Stoke Mandville, England.
Various competitive opportunities available for these populations
at national and international levels are discussed. Available from
International Rehabilitation Film Library, 20 East 40th Street, New
York, NY 10018.

4. Not Just a Spectator

16 mm, color, 26 minutes. Shows the many and sometimes unlikely
activities that challenge, give personal satisfaction, and provide
pleasure to a great number of people with different handicapping
conditions. Available from Town and Country Productions, 21 Cheyne
Row, Chelsea, London, 3W3 5HP. Available in the United States from
International Rehabilitation Film Library, 20 West 40th Street, New
York, NY 10018.

5. In Search of Balance

16 mm, color, sound, 25 minutes. Narrated by Eddie Albert; depicts
importance and meaning of leisure in our lives. National Recreation
and Park Association, 1001 North Kent Street, Arlington, VA 22209.

6. <u>Is it Le/zher or Lezh/er?</u>

16 mm, color, sound, 31 minutes. Describes how the public in general
and professionals in particular interpret the meaning of leisure and
recreation. Films and Video for Health Sciences, Pennsylvania State
University, Audio-Visual Services, Special Services Building, University
Park, PA 16802.

7. <u>Grow Older--Feel Younger</u>

16 mm, color, sound, motivational film, 10 minutes. Developed as
part of the "Active People Over 60" program. National Association
for Human Development, 1750 Pennsylvania NW, Washington, DC 20006.

APPENDIX B

Equipment List

Following is a list of materials needed for activities in the recreation units:

ALL UNITS - ACTIVITY PLAN 1

pencils with erasers
Recreation Interest Survey sheets
unit descriptions

LITERATURE

writing paper
pencils
variety of reading materials (books, plays, Bible, etc.)
envelopes, stamps (for mailing a letter)
newspapers
current news magazine such as Time or Newsweek
dictionary
records or tapes of a variety of musical selections
phonograph and/or tape player

HOBBIES

resource materials on indoor gardening
variety of plant containers
soil or potting mix
small plant or plant cutting
simple gardening tools
resource materials on bird watching
resource materials on astronomy
tape player or phonograph
variety of records or tapes of music
old newspapers to protect work space

jigsaw puzzles
paper, pencils
dictionary (optional)

GAMES

deck of cards (several decks)
lapboard
golf club, preferably a putter
golf balls (3-5)
set of dominoes
checkers
masking tape
pens
magic markers
pencil and paper
4 shoe boxes

CRAFTS

scissors or pinking shears
sewing needles
thread
embroidery floss
ribbon
material scraps
nylon hose
clear plastic wood spray finish
Exacto knife
paring knife
old jars of various sizes (pickle jars, peanut butter jars, baby food
  jars, etc.)
white glue
acrylic paints
variety of paint brushes
measuring tape
yarn
corks
plain wrapping paper
drawing paper (nonslick surface)
water-based block printing ink
measuring cup or utensil
assorted sewing notions
old socks

zippers
bread flour (all-purpose)
salt
wax paper
newspaper
variety of magazine pictures
baking sheet
cookie cutters
pizza cutter
toothpicks
rolling pin
plastic bags
mixing bowls
pancake turner
pot holders
some type of sealer (shellac, varnish, polyurethane, lacquer, etc.)
powdered soap or detergent
tin cans or oatmeal cartons to hold paint brushes
felt-tip pens

REMEMBERING THE PAST

travel magazines
tape recorder and blank tapes
cloth pieces for book covers
ribbons
stapler with staples or fasteners
iron-on seam binding
scissors, thread, needle, and thimble
iron

Leader Training Program

1. Introduction (35 minutes)

   a. Introduction of training staff and leaders
   b. Introduction to the program

2. Characteristics/Needs of the Elderly (30 minutes)

   a. Reasons why some elderly are home-centered
   b. Common problems/needs of the home-centered

3. Learning about Recreation (1 hour)

   a. Basic concepts of recreation
   b. Value of recreation to leader; to elder

4. Leader and Elder Assignments (30 minutes)

   a. Pair leaders and elder participants
   b. Discuss initial phone contact

5. Learning about Leading Activities (1 hour)

   a. General principles of leading activities
   b. Introduction of the activity plan format

6. Conducting Sessions (2 hours)

   a. Role play various types of sessions

      1) Activity modification
      2) Leadership principles
      3) Resource materials

      b.   Role play special situations or concerns

            1) Emergency procedures
            2) Motivation
            3) Ending a session
            4) Behavior problems
            5) Confidentiality

7. Leader and Elder Meeting (15 minutes)

      a.   Discuss initial phone contact
      b.   Prepare for first session

8. Conducting the First Session (1 hour, 15 minutes)

      a.   Discuss Leisure Interest survey
      b.   Role play session (1)

9. Follow-up Discussion (25 minutes)

      a.   Review resource materials
      b.   Discuss initial session problems and successes
      c.   General questions and answers

10. Training Wrap-Up (30 minutes)

      a.   Evaluate training program
      b.   Arrange weekly meeting of leaders
      c.   Award certificate of training and tote basket
      d.   Pep talk and last minute instructions

Certificate of Training

has successfully completed training in the delivery of

Activities for the Elderly

Program Director/Trainer

Date

APPENDIX D

Job Description

POSITION TITLE: Recreation Leader

PURPOSE OF THE POSITION: To conduct a session of at least 1 hour a week with an elderly person and conduct recreation activities with this person.

POSITION RESPONSIBILITIES: Complete training program.

Meet one time per week, for a period of 9 weeks on the day arranged, or call if an emergency should prevent the session and set a new date.

Record contact hours and meet with the program coordinator as requested.

Be alert to other needs or problems of the elderly person and report these to the coordinator.

Report to the coordinator if a situation should arise in which you cannot continue as a leader in order that a replacement may be found.

Meet bi-monthly with other leaders to share items, ideas, problems, etc.

Participate in a follow-up social gathering at the completion of the program.

QUALIFICATIONS: Liking for the elderly.

                               Honesty.

                               Dependability.

                               Willingness to receive training.

                               Ability to arrange for own transportation.

                               Respect for confidentality.

                               Ability to relate to elderly people on
                               a one-to-one basis.

TERM OF POSITION: For 9 weeks or as long as the relationship
                               continues satisfactorily to both the
                               leader and the participant.

HOURS: Except for training, hours are by
                               arrangement with the elder. Preparation
                               for and conducting a session requires
                               approximately 2 hours. The leaders also
                               meet on a bi-monthly basis for an hour.

REIMBURSEMENT: Leaders do not receive pay for their
                               time commitment.

                               Food is provided during training sessions
                               when appropriate.

                               Reimbursement for transportation costs
                               and minor supplies can be arranged with
                               the coordinator.

                               A certificate of training is given to
                               each leader after completing training.